THE

BLENDER
SHAKER
BOTTLE
RECIPE BOOK

THE

BLENDER
SHAKER
BOTTLE
RECIPE BOOK

Over **125** Protein Powder Shake
Recipes Everyone Can Use for Vitality,
Optimum Nutrition and Restoration
– For Blender Bottle, Cup & Shaker
Bottle with Ball

BETH HARPER

ALBRIGHT PRESS
contact@albrightpress.info

DISCLAIMER

The publisher and author make no representations or warranties with respect to the accuracy or completeness of the contents of this work and specially disclaim all warranties, including warranties without limitation warranties of fitness for a particular purpose. No warranties may be created or extended by sales or promotions. The information and strategies herein may not be suitable for every situation. This material is sold with the understanding that the author or publisher is not engaged in rendering medical, legal, or other professional advice or services. If professional help is required, the services of a competent professional should be sought. Neither the publisher nor the author shall be liable for damages arising here from. The fact that an individual or organisation is referred to in this work as a citation and/or possible source of further information or resource does not mean the author or the publisher endorses the information of the individual or organisation that they/it may provide or recommend.

Many of the designations used by manufacturers and sellers to distinguish their products are claimed as trademarks. Any and all product names referenced within this book are the trademarks of their respective owners. None of these owners have sponsored, endorsed or approved this book. Always read all information provided by the manufacturer's product labels or manuals before using their products. The author and publisher are not responsible for product claims made by manufacturers.

Table of Contents

POWER-UP YOUR DAY—ENERGIZE YOUR LIFE!

Hi, I'm Beth and I'm in love with two inseparable sweethearts. My blender shaker bottle and protein shakes! In fact, I should really say "my blender shaker bottles" because I do not own just one, but four of these shaker bottles. Why four? Well, I use a bottle specifically for water-based protein shakes and I use another for my milk-based shakes. The other two bottles are kept in reserve, so that in case one of the other bottles gets ruined, I can quickly replace it. I would never want to miss having my sweethearts around!

To be honest, I wasn't always into protein shakes. As I can recall, it was my husband, Les, who has always been a protein shake lover and was always blending one of his favorite concoctions. Apart from being unenthused by his boring shakes (by the way I always told him that they were great), I also hated the fact that his blending routine had made me into a permanent blender washer-girl. Les never had the time to wash the blender. I mean never ever. He always had an excuse to do something else.

Quite remarkably though, my husband's daily protein shake routine helped him to get rid of his 10 year beer belly! And, that's when protein shakes got my attention. I was interested in anything that could help me lose my post-baby bump which has stubbornly remained after 6 years despite my regular 30-minute abs workout. So, eventually I joined Les. Now, considering that I was already feeling overwhelmed with his blender regime, I wanted to find an easy way out. The blender shaker bottle was my game-changer. By using the shaker bottle, I found that cleaning up was a breeze, in fact it is also dishwasher safe. Whew! Subsequently, I started to make daily protein shakes in my shaker bottle by using some interesting and healthy ingredients. I did some research, stretched my imagination and the results were very encouraging. I ended up making healthy and delicious shakes beyond my wildest dreams. One of the best parts is that I lost three quarter of my post-baby bump and I'm feeling full of energy. Now, I just have a small (not so obvious) paunch now. Good for me! I can live with that. By the way, Les couldn't keep his mouth shut about my delectable shakes. Now, occasionally even his workmate, Frank, keeps looking forward to another of my signature shakes.

Overtime, I have solidified my shaker bottle shake-making experience and began to share my creative recipes with more family and friends. And what a journey it has been! I have gotten countless compliments for my intriguing shakes. Today, it is with much passion and confidence that I share my recipes with you and others around the globe. So, I encourage you to start using your shaker bottle to make these delicious shakes recipes—energize your life!

PROTEIN POWDER FOR EVERYONE

There's more to using protein powder than building muscles. Broadly speaking, almost everyone can use a protein powder supplement to enhance their health. By using protein powders the right way, it will help to provide the body with optimum protein nutrition. Our body uses protein as the vital building blocks which support the growth and restoration of muscle tissue whenever we take part in any kind of physical activity. Moreover, it has been found that protein powders enter the bloodstream much quicker than other animal protein sources such as eggs or meats, and without the added stress of worrying about high fat and cholesterol levels. Interesting, isn't it? Therefore, for extra energy and a quick protein boost for general good health, having a protein powder shake is a great option.

Additionally, many weight loss experts have agreed that while using protein powder shakes to help curb the appetite; there is also an avoidance of muscle loss syndrome. Muscle loss often occurs as people lose body fat and often results in the muscles becoming less toned and more floppy. Consequently, other health related issues such as unusual tiredness, weakness and even malnutrition may also become a part of the spiraling effects of losing muscle tissues. Thus, considering the overall benefits, protein powder shakes could be an essential part of a healthy weight loss program.

PROTEIN POWDER FOR CHILDREN

Maybe, you've wondered about whether or not protein powder is good for kids. Well, maybe you didn't know this, but quite a number of infant formulas contain protein powder as an ingredient. Furthermore, medical and scientific studies have revealed that protein powder can significantly strengthen a child's immune system and help them to better resist different illnesses. This is because good quality protein powders contain both antioxidant and immune boosting properties which are all essential for the healthy growth and development of children. Unless a child has some known dairy sensitivity, whey protein powders are usually among the best quality protein powders on the market. Good quality whey protein powder should be manufactured by a reputable facility which abides by FDA standards.

PROTEIN POWDER FOR WOMEN

When it comes to protein powder benefits for women, the fat loss factor carries much value. By acting as an appetite control mechanism, protein powder works well in curbing food cravings. Furthermore, many women have successfully used protein powder to lose weight, gain weight and increase muscle mass. Another important issue for most women especially as they age is bone loss. However, with an adequate intake of protein, there is usually considerable reduction in the risk of bone loss related issues such as joint problems or osteoporosis in women. By incorporating protein shakes in the daily diet, women will be able to easily increase their protein intake for better health.

PROTEIN POWDER FOR MEN

The words 'protein powder' and 'muscle builders' have become more and more synonymous. For ages, men have been using protein powders to increase lean muscle mass. Whether it is before or after a vigorous workout, protein powders have truly been a muscle builder's best friend. Studies have indicated that as muscle builders aim to preserve their muscles with protein powders, they also lose body fat. Thus, for a flabby-free fat loss experience and well-toned muscles, a protein shake really goes a long way. Besides, not only does a healthy glass of protein powder shake help to tone the muscles, it also helps to strengthen it. Strengthening of the muscles has been shown to work particularly well for men who have a protein powder shake both before and after their weightlifting session.

WHY YOU NEED THIS RECIPE BOOK

This shake recipe book is not just for body builders! Instead, it is for everyone who wants to make healthy and delicious protein shakes with their blender shaker bottle or cup. The book is specially created with a unique collection of over 125 healthy and easy protein powder recipes all themed in eight (8) different categories. Furthermore, these protein shake recipes are all calories counted and are created to support your specific health goals. So whether you want to build muscles, adjust your weight, or simply maintain good health, you're sure to find some interesting recipes in this book. Even more, in this book you will find blender shaker bottle recipes that will:

- Support your work-out program
- Help you to lose or gain weight
- Increase and maintain lean muscle mass
- Boost your metabolism
- Enhance the overall health of your whole family
- Increase your energy levels
- Lower insulin levels
- Increase your protein intake for maintaining optimum health

Considering all this, your shaker bottle journey would not be complete without trying these inspiring protein shake recipes. With the specially selected ingredients and easy directions, you'll be successful in creating healthy and flavorful protein shakes within minutes. Start making tasty protein shakes that you and your family will love!

CHOOSING THE BEST PROTEIN POWDER

There are many manufacturers of protein powder on the market, but not all are created equal. Allergies tend to be among the most common issue that concern most folks who are getting into protein powders. These allergy concerns may arise based on the type of protein elements like milk lactose, soy, casein or eggs. Another common allergy concern relates to artificial ingredients, that some would like to avoid. The good news is that in each of these cases of concern, there are usually many product alternatives from which to choose.

Despite the wide range of protein powders presently offered on the market, the variations boil right down to a couple of characteristics:

- The type of protein used
- Different kind of flavors and sweeteners used
- Value per serving or per gram of protein
- Extra ingredients that may have been included to enhance the product's overall benefits

PROTEIN TYPES

The types of protein that is commonly utilized in protein powders may be divided into two (2) categories: animal derived protein and vegetable derived protein. Animal derived protein comes in the form of protein derivatives like casein, egg white protein, goat's milk and whey protein. Vegetable derived protein comes in the form of rice, pea, hemp and soy proteins.

From the standpoint of good nutrition and taste, proteins from animal sources are more popular and of a better quality than protein from vegetable sources. Whey protein is the most commonly used type of animal protein, while pea, rice and soy proteins are the most commonly used types of vegetable protein. The vegetable protein sources have been most commonly used by those who are a part of a plant-based eating regime, those who are seeking to optimize their heart health and those who want to regulate hormone imbalance.

Whey Protein

Whey protein is a milk derivative which has two varieties: whey isolate and whey concentrate. The full protein percentage of whole milk is divided into 80% casein protein and 20% whey protein. When it comes to protein powders, there's no doubt that whey protein is the most popularly used protein. This is mainly because of it superior quality, great taste, affordability and its immune boosting benefits.

Each variety of whey protein powder has its own unique benefits. The whey isolate version is quite low on fat and this feature makes it an ideal pick for those who are following a low-fat lifestyle. Interestingly, whey isolate is usually an ideal pick for some persons with some degree of lactose sensitivities. Comparatively, whey concentrate tends be more reasonably priced per protein gram. It is also known to be low on lactose levels, low fat and low in carbs.

Milk Protein or Casein

Casein protein is also a milk derivative and is also commonly referred to as milk protein or calcium caseinate. Because casein accounts for 80% of whole milk, this also means that most of the protein in milk is actually casein. By comparing, casein protein with whey protein even though they are similar in taste, one major difference is that casein is digested slowly while whey is digested quickly. Consider that some protein powders may offer both casein and whey in the ingredients, while others may be whey only or casein only. Either way, it all boils down to consumer preference and choice as both are found to offer useful health benefits.

Egg White Protein

For decades, our ancestors had used egg white as the readily available protein source for those who were following a dairy-free lifestyle. Back then, and even now, one of the main drawbacks to egg white protein has been its raw aftertaste and higher cost when compared to other milk based protein alternatives. Nevertheless, many folks have resorted to egg white protein for its cholesterol-free, dairy-free, low carb and low fat benefits.

Vegetable Proteins

Understandably, vegetable proteins have always been the protein choice for those who are following a plant-based lifestyle. The most popular vegetable proteins are: pea, soy and rice protein. For the benefits of well needed amino acids, soy protein and hemp protein are clear winners among the different vegetable proteins. Additionally, despite its overpowering taste, soy protein is a clear choice for those who are seeking to capitalize on its isoflavone, antioxidant and heart health benefits. Consider that there is tasty soy protein available on the market for those who want to dodge its prominent flavor.

PROTEIN POWDER FLAVOURS AND SWEETENERS

When it comes to flavors and sweeteners, there is a protein powder for everyone, no matter your taste, age or lifestyle preference. Protein powder types can be found with artificial or natural flavors and sweeteners or a combination of both. Options are also available for those who don't wish to have added sweeteners or flavors in their protein powder. Note that the availability of various sweeteners and flavors does not alter the protein powder's nutritional value.

PROTEIN POWDER COST

It's a tough call trying to compare the prices of different

protein powders based on the wide spectrum of factors that should be considered. However, you should bear in mind that protein powder prices may vary according to protein types, flavors and sweeteners, nutritional enhancers and a wide range of other possible additives. Whichever protein powder you have chosen, usually it works out to be much cheaper if you purchase the largest available size.

PROTEIN POWDER ENHANCERS

Natural and artificial sweeteners and flavors are not the only enhancements that are typically added to protein powders. Additional enhancements are often added to improve the taste, improve consumer experience, or increase the nutrient base of a particular product. For example, soy lecithin or lecithin as it is commonly called is added to some protein powders as a means of lump reduction. Moreover, soy lecithin is also known to improve brain and heart health. Other beneficial and popular protein powder enhancers include amino acids, digestive enzymes, vitamins and minerals, good fats and even carbs. In the end, consumer preference plays a big factor when it comes to enhancers. Whenever choosing enhancers, it is best to choose those that will improve your personal health situation.

MAKING A HEALTHY PROTEIN SHAKE

Generally speaking, protein shakes can be a healthy choice if you're trying to lose weight, build muscles or just simply improve your health. This is particularly true if you make it yourself and you know exactly what ingredients are added. A serving of freshly made protein shake is not only satisfying, but it will also help to curb your appetite and keep you feeling full for longer.

For a long time, many people have become accustomed to making their healthy homemade shakes with a high speed blender instead of a blender shaker bottle. Note that one of the main differences between using the two is that the shaker bottle functions more like a mixer instead of a blender. In this case, while the blender is able to grind solid ingredients such as ice, nuts, chopped fruits and vegetables, the shaker bottle does not grind. Nevertheless, the shaker bottle is able to easily mix even the thickest ingredients. With this in mind, easy and inspiring ideas are always wanted for making healthy shakes with the shaker bottle. If you've never made a healthy protein shake in your shaker bottle before, give it a go, you'll be surprised by how easy it can be. It all starts by ensuring that you have a variety of healthy shaker bottle ingredients in your pantry.

CONSIDERING SHAKE SUBSTITUTES AND ADDITIVES

Making homemade shakes should be fun! For this reason, these shakes can be easily tweaked to suit your personal preferences and imagination. Here follows some listed ingredients of shake substitutes and ingredient suggestions.

- Substitute skim milk with: unsweetened almond milk, unsweetened coconut water, soy milk, rice milk, hemp milk, pure filtered water and organic unsweetened coconut milk.
- Substitute juices with: unsweetened coconut water, carrot juice, orange juice, pomegranate juice, pineapple juice, peach juice, cranberry juice, strawberry juice, cherry juice, raspberry juice, mixed berry juice, strawberry nectar and pure filtered water.
- Substitute mashed banana for: mashed avocado, apple sauce and kiwi sauce.
- Substitute yogurt with: cherry yogurt, banana cream pie yogurt, triple berry yogurt, blueberry yogurt, lemon yogurt, strawberry yogurt, key lime yogurt, peach yogurt and piña colada yogurt.
- Substitute ground nuts and seeds with: almond meal, ground chia seeds, ground flax seeds, hazel nut meal, pistachio nut meal, pecan meal, ground oats and low-fat granola.
- Substitute nut butters with: pecan butter, peanut butter, almond butter, coconut butter and walnut butter.
- Use healthy and natural shake additives or enhancers: cayenne pepper, pomegranate juice, aloe vera juice, avocado, hemp powder, acai powder, bee pollen, nutritional yeast, chia seeds, coconut oil, flax oil, ground ginger, maca root powder, wheat germ, fresh or powdered wheatgrass juice, yogurt, kefir, organic spinach powder, organic beet powder and spirulina powder.
- Use the taste and flavor enhancers (note that some of these may contain combinations of natural and artificial ingredients and may change the flavor or consistency of

your shake) : coconut extract, vanilla extract, instant vanilla pudding (sugar free or regular), peppermint extract, instant coffee, butterscotch pudding mix, cherry extract, coconut cream pudding mix, banana extract, banana flavor pudding mix, hazelnut extract, oreo pudding mix, French vanilla creamer, instant chocolate pudding mix, sugar-free lemon pudding mix, sugar-free orange gelatin powder, pistachio pudding mix and sugar-free strawberry gelatin powder.

SHAKER BOTTLE SHAKE MAKING POINTERS

Getting the most out of your homemade shaker bottle shake is important. You may find this section to be particularly helpful if you are new to making shakes with your shaker bottle or if you want to understand how you can get the most benefit from every sip. Hence, in order to help you get the most benefits from drinking these shakes and to avoid some typical mistakes, I'll share some personal guidelines:

- To make my shake routine much easier, I usually make my shake shopping list about a week or so earlier based on the recipes that I intend to make.
- When I am ready to drink my shake, I always shake my shaker bottle well, as ingredient separation may sometimes occur.
- I chew my shakes to aid digestion and avoid bloating, while also sipping slowly.
- If I don't want to put on a few pounds or build muscles, I never drink my shakes with a meal.
- I don't eat anything approximately 25-30 minutes before or 25-30 minutes after I've finished drinking my shake. This helps to support proper digestion and to ensure that I get the most nutritional benefit out of my shake.
- If I decide to add more ingredients to my shake, I usually try to keep it simple. By doing this, I am able to avoid

digestive upsets and preserve certain flavors.
- I stick to my favorite delicious shakes and switch whenever I feel like trying something new. By doing this, I am able to shorten my shopping list and also look forward to the next shake. Taste usually appeals to everyone differently, so it is almost natural that you'll soon come up with your own favorite recipes as well.
- I never mix hot liquids in my shaker bottle.
- I prefer unsweetened or freshly squeezed juices in order to ensure that I am getting natural vitamins and minerals from my shakes and to ensure that I avoid hidden sugars.
- I never drink too much shake. Whenever I am full, that's the time I stop drinking.
- I don't use left-over shake from my shaker bottle, unless it was stored in a separate container in the refrigerator.
- Even though my blender shaker bottle is dishwasher safe, I usually hand wash the lid. This may help to avoid the cracking of the lid due to frequent dishwashing.
- I always secure my bottle with the lid properly, before I decide to give it a good shake. So snap it before you shake it.
- I do not encourage placing your shaker bottle in the freezer.

FOOLPROOF SHAKE MAKING STEPS

Even though these shakes are quick and easy to make, the following super easy steps will help to ensure that you will always make the perfect protein shake.

Step 1: Add the liquid ingredients in your shaker bottle first, followed by your protein powder of choice, secure with the lid and shake well. This will help to make your shake lump-free and as smooth as possible.

Step 2: Add all other additives and enhancers that you want to include in the shake, secure again with the lid and shake well while ensuring that all ingredients are properly combined.

Drink and enjoy. Also, note that if you wish to add crushed ice to your shake, you may do so after completing these mentioned steps.

HOW TO USE THIS RECIPE BOOK

Before you begin shake making, you should ensure that you have all the necessary ingredients. By doing this, you'll be able to approach the recipes with confidence and achieve perfect results every time. After choosing a recipe, you should follow the specific recipe directions. As time goes by, you'll be able to come up with your own inspiring, tasty and healthy shake recipes. Furthermore, for variety, ease of use and individual protein requirements, this book is conveniently themed into eight (8) different recipe categories:

EVERYDAY SHAKES

These recipes consist of a largest variety of healthy shake ingredients that can be used any time of day by those who just simple want to maintain their weight and improve their health. These shakes are specifically created to meet your need for variety and contain a single scoop (28 grams) of protein powder per serving.

Daily Recommendation: 1 serving daily of protein shake at least 30 minutes after a meal.

MUSCLE BUILDING SHAKES

These recipes consist of a variety of healthy shake ingredients and are specifically created for those who are involved in muscle training and strengthening. This section is the perfect pick for muscle builders and for those looking for post-workout or pre-workout shakes. These shake contain a double scoop (56 grams) of protein powder per serving. In case you want to power-down a bit, you may use a single scoop (28g) for these shakes.

Daily Recommendation: 1 serving daily of protein shake before and/or after a workout and with or without a meal.

WEIGHT LOSS SHAKES

These recipes consist of a variety of healthy shake ingredients and are specifically created for those who want to lose weight. This section contains recipes with the perfect pick of fat burning ingredients and contains a single scoop (28 grams) of protein powder per serving.

Daily Recommendation: 1 serving daily of protein shake in replacement of breakfast, lunch or dinner.

LOW SUGAR & LOW CARB SHAKES

These recipes consist of a variety of healthy shake ingredients for those who want to consume less sugar and fewer carbs. These shakes are also specifically created to meet the needs of those who are diabetic and contain a single scoop (28 grams) of protein powder per serving.

Daily Recommendation: 1 serving daily of protein shake at least 30 minutes after a meal.

KIDS SHAKES

These recipes consist of a variety of healthy shake ingredients that are likely to please even the pickiest kid. These shakes are specifically created to support a healthy immune system and overall good health of children. Each recipe contains half scoop (14 grams) of protein powder per serving.

Daily Recommendation: 1 serving daily of protein shake with a meal or at least 30 minutes after a meal. If you want to avoid weight gaining, it is best to serve the shake after a meal instead of with the meal.

BRAIN HEALTHY SHAKES

These recipes consist of a variety of healthy shake ingredients that are in support of healthy brain functions. Each recipe contains a single scoop (28 grams) of protein powder per serving. Note that these shakes can easily be converted to create healthy brain shakes for kids by using half the amount of protein powder (14 grams).

Daily Recommendation: 1 serving daily of protein shake at least 30 minutes after a meal.

WEIGHT GAIN SHAKES

These recipes consist of a variety of healthy shake ingredients that are created specifically to support weight gain. This section is perfect for those who have some kind of eating disorder or those who just simply want to put on a few pounds. Each recipe contains a single scoop (28 grams) of protein powder per serving.

Daily Recommendation: 1-2 servings of protein shake daily with a meal.

DINNER SHAKES

These recipes consist of a variety of healthy shake ingredients that can be used specifically at dinner or by those who just simple want to maintain their weight and improve their health. These dinner shakes have moderate amount of carbohydrate, low fat and other carefully chosen ingredients that do not promote excess build up or storage of fat. These shakes are also created to meet your need for variety and contain a single scoop (28 grams) of protein powder per serving.

Daily Recommendation: 1 servings of protein shake at dinner time. If you want to avoid gaining weight, it is best to serve the dinner shake after a meal instead of with the meal. However, if you want to lose weight, you may have a dinner shake in replacement of dinner.

READY, SET, SHAKE!

I have spent a lot of time to bring these recipes to perfection, but sometimes it's impossible to catch it all. So, if you have any questions about this publication, please send me an email at: beth@albrightpress.info. I would be very appreciative of your feedback and I will respond to you as quickly as possible.

Here follows a measurement guide for easy US and UK measurement conversions:

A QUICK MEASUREMENT GUIDE

Liquids
1 tsp = 6ml
1 tbsp = 15ml
1/8 cup = 30ml
1/4 cup = 60ml
1/2 cup = 120ml
1 cup = 240ml

Dried ingredients
1 tsp = 5g
1 tbsp = 15g
1oz = 28g
1 cup flour = 150g
1 cup caster sugar = 225g

1 cup icing sugar = 115g
1 cup brown sugar = 175g
1 cup sultanas = 200g

Nut Butter
1/8 cup = 30g
1/4 cup = 55g
1/3 cup = 75g
1/2 cup = 115g
2/3 cup = 150g
3/4 cup = 170g
1 cup = 225g

Live a healthier life with these protein shakes. Now get ready, set and shake.

Let's start shaking!

EVERYDAY PROTEIN SHAKES

Banana Nut Twist

This energy-giving shake is packed with rich proteins, antioxidants and healthy fats. This may become a morning favorite before you know it.

Makes: *1 Serving*
Preparation Time: *10 Minutes*
391 Calories per serving

Ingredients

- 1 cup (240ml) unsweetened Almond Milk (or use your favorite dairy or non-dairy milk)
- 1 scoop (28g) Protein Powder (use your favorite)
- 1 tablespoon (15g) raw organic Nut Butter (pecan, almond or coconut)
- 1 large ripe Banana, mashed
- ½ teaspoon (2.5g) Cinnamon Powder
- ¼ teaspoon (1g) Ground Ginger

Directions

Pour the almond milk and protein powder in your blender bottle and shake well until the protein powder is completely dissolved.

Add the remaining ingredients to the protein powder mixture and shake thoroughly until all ingredients are evenly blended together.

Note: calories may vary slightly due to brands and other recipe modifications.

Cheery Chocolate Heart

Enjoy this rich and creamy chocolaty shake loaded with rich fiber and omega 3. Enjoy the powerful cardiovascular health benefits s from the flaxseed which is enriched with omega fatty acids.

Makes: 1 *Serving*
Preparation Time: 5 *Minutes*
281 Calories per serving

Ingredients

- 1 cup (240ml) Skim Milk (or use your favorite dairy or non-dairy milk)
- 1 scoop (28g) Chocolate Protein Powder
- ½ cup (120ml) Chocolate Yogurt
- 1 tablespoon (15g) Ground Flaxseed
- Pinch of Sea Salt (optional)

Directions

Pour the milk and protein powder in your blender bottle

and shake well until the protein powder is completely dissolved.

Add the remaining ingredients to the protein powder mixture and shake thoroughly until all ingredients are evenly blended together.

Note: calories may vary slightly due to brands and other recipe modifications.

Granola Punch

This very tasty and healthy shake will keep you full for hours. Apart from being fiber rich and protein rich shake that you may enjoy in the morning, you may also have it whenever you need a heavy protein meal.

Makes: 1 Serving
Preparation Time: 5 Minutes
411 Calories per serving

Ingredients

- 1 cup (240ml) Skim Milk (or use your favorite dairy or non-dairy milk)
- 1 scoop (28g) Protein Powder (use your favorite)
- 1 tablespoon (15g) Natural Peanut Butter
- ¼ teaspoon (1g) Ground Nutmeg
- ¼ cup (38g) Low-fat Granola
- Natural Stevia (or sweetener of your choice) to taste

Directions

Pour the milk and protein powder in your blender bottle and shake well until the protein powder is completely dissolved.

Add the remaining ingredients to the protein powder mixture and shake thoroughly until all ingredients are evenly blended together.

Note: calories may vary slightly due to brands and other recipe modifications.

Spiced Apple Parade

This apple spice shake is gives a nice twist to a healthy protein breakfast without packing on too many calories. It is quick-fix for one of those busy mornings and will surely satisfy your taste buds.

Makes: *1 Serving*
Preparation Time: *5 Minutes*
179 Calories per serving

Ingredients

- ¾ cup (240ml) Filtered Water
- 1 scoop (28g) Vanilla Protein Powder
- ½ cup (120ml) Unsweetened Applesauce
- ½ teaspoon (2.5g) Cinnamon Powder
- ¼ teaspoon (1g) Ground Nutmeg
- Natural Stevia or preferred sweetener to taste (optional)

Directions

Pour the water and protein powder in your blender bottle and shake well until the protein powder is completely dissolved.

Add the remaining ingredients to the protein powder mixture and shake thoroughly until all ingredients are evenly

blended together.

Note: calories may vary slightly due to brands and other recipe modifications.

Greek Vanilla Orange

There's nothing like getting that extra Vitamin C boost with your protein shake. With a slight gingery background taste and a rich creamy texture, this shake has pleased many hearts. Enjoy.

Makes: 1 Serving
Preparation Time: 10 Minutes
322.5 Calories per serving

Ingredients
- 1 cup (240ml) freshly squeezed Orange Juice
- 1 scoop (28g) Protein Powder
- ½ cup (120ml) Plain Yogurt
- 1 teaspoon (6ml) Vanilla Extract
- ½ teaspoon (2.5g) Ground Ginger

Directions
Pour the orange juice and protein powder in your blender bottle and shake well until the protein powder is completely dissolved.

Add the remaining ingredients to the protein powder mixture and shake thoroughly until all ingredients are evenly blended together.

Note: calories may vary slightly due to brands and other recipe

modifications.

Flax-Berry

Have some extra time to mash or puree some blueberries? Every minute that you'll use to prepare this flax-berry shake is well worth it. Enjoy the rich antioxidant benefits coupled with the healthy fiber and proteins in every sip.

Makes: 1 Serving
Preparation Time: 5 Minutes
275 Calories per serving

Ingredients

- 1 cup (240ml) unsweetened Almond Milk (or use your favorite dairy or non-dairy milk)
- 1 scoop (28g) Protein Powder
- ½ cup (120ml) Blueberry Yogurt
- 1 tablespoon (15g) Ground Flaxseed

Directions

Pour the almond milk and protein powder in your blender bottle and shake well until the protein powder is completely dissolved.

Add the remaining ingredients to the protein powder mixture and shake thoroughly until all ingredients are evenly blended together.

Note: calories may vary slightly due to brands and other recipe modifications.

Pumpkin Pleasures

This delicious pumpkin shake will be very comforting to the stomach. With these simple shake ingredients you'll be fully powered to have a good day. Enjoy this for a nice weekend breakfast shake or whenever you wish.

Makes: *1 Serving*
Preparation Time: *5 Minutes*
278.5 Calories per serving

Ingredients

- 1 cup (240ml) Skim Milk (or use your favorite dairy or non-dairy milk)
- 1 scoop (28g) Protein Powder
- ½ cup (115g) of cooked, mashed and cooled Pumpkin or Pumpkin Puree
- ½ teaspoon (2.5g) Cinnamon Powder
- ¼ teaspoon (1g) Ground Nutmeg
- 1 teaspoon (6ml) Vanilla Extract
- Natural Stevia or preferred sweetener to taste
- Pinch of Sea Salt

Directions

Pour the milk and protein powder in your blender bottle and shake well until the protein powder is completely dissolved.

Add the remaining ingredients to the protein powder mixture and shake thoroughly until all ingredients are evenly blended together.

Note: calories may vary slightly due to brands and other recipe modifications.

Gingery Pomegranate Delight

Enjoy the health benefits of this super food pomegranate shake which is packed with antioxidants and protein goodness. With a rich earthy taste in every sip, you'll know that you're drinking something healthy.

Makes: 1 Serving
Preparation Time: 5 Minutes
438 Calories per serving

Ingredients

- ¾ cup (240ml) fresh unsweetened Pomegranate Juice
- 1 scoop (28g) Protein Powder
- 1 cup (240ml) Strawberry Yogurt
- 1 teaspoon (5g) Ground Ginger

Directions

Pour the pomegranate juice and protein powder in your blender bottle and shake well until the protein powder is completely dissolved.

Add the remaining ingredients to the protein powder mixture and shake thoroughly until all ingredients are evenly blended together.

Note: calories may vary slightly due to brands and other recipe modifications.

Coffee Creek

Now you can have your coffee with your protein shake all in your blender bottle. So, whether you are a coffee lover or not; this delicious coffee shake may surely tickle your fancy. It gets its fruity taste from the banana and is enriched with proteins from both the yogurt and the protein powder.

Makes: *1 Serving*
Preparation Time: *10 Minutes*
428 Calories per serving

Ingredients

- *1 cup (240ml) brewed Coffee, cooled and chilled
- 1 scoop (28g) Protein Powder
- 1 cup (240ml) Plain Yogurt
- 1 large ripe Banana, mashed
- 1 tablespoon (15g) Ground Flaxseed
- ½ teaspoon (2.5g) Cinnamon Powder
- ¼ teaspoon (1g) Ground Nutmeg
- Natural Stevia or preferred sweetener to taste (optional)
- Pinch of Sea Salt

Directions

Pour the coffee and protein powder in your blender bottle and shake well until the protein powder is completely dissolved.

Add the remaining ingredients to the protein powder mixture and shake thoroughly until all ingredients are evenly blended together.

*Brew coffee overnight and place in the refrigerator to chill for best results

Note: calories may vary slightly due to brands and other recipe modifications.

Nutty Island Mix

Pecan meal is used in this shake to give it that rich nutty flavor, however may substitute pecan for your favorite ground nuts, such as almonds, pistachio or walnuts. This tasty shake is packed with fiber and healthy fats to enrich your protein experience.

Makes: 1 Serving
Preparation Time: 10 Minutes
216 Calories per serving

Ingredients

- 1 cup (240ml) unsweetened Almond Milk (or use your favorite dairy or non-dairy milk)
- 1 scoop (28g) Vanilla Protein Powder
- ¼ cup (38g) Pecan Meal
- ¼ teaspoon (1g) Ground Nutmeg
- 1 teaspoon (6ml) Organic Hazelnut Extract
- Natural Stevia or preferred sweetener to taste
- Pinch of Sea Salt

Directions

Pour the almond milk and protein powder in your blender bottle and shake well until the protein powder is completely dissolved.

Add the remaining ingredients to the protein powder mixture and shake thoroughly until all ingredients are evenly blended together.

*The ground nuts can be presoaked overnight in about ½ cup (120ml) of water for better results

Note: calories may vary slightly due to brands and other recipe modifications.

Coco-Pine Craze

Coconut and pineapple could be described as a perfect match. In this shake, coconut milk and pineapple juice is combined with the super food power of chia seeds to deliver a protein shake of bursting nutritional goodness.

Makes: *1 Serving*
Preparation Time: *20 Minutes*
336.5 Calories per serving

Ingredients

- ½ cup (120ml) unsweetened Organic Coconut Milk (or use your favorite dairy or non-dairy milk)
- ½ cup (120ml) fresh unsweetened Pineapple Juice
- 1 scoop (28g) Protein Powder
- ½ cup (120ml) Piña Colada Yogurt
- 1 tablespoon (15g) Ground Chia Seeds
- ½ teaspoon (2.5g) Cinnamon Powder
- Natural Stevia or preferred sweetener to taste (optional)
- Pinch of Sea Salt

Directions

Pour the coconut milk, pineapple juice and protein powder in your blender bottle and shake well until the protein powder is completely dissolved.

Add the remaining ingredients to the protein powder mixture and shake thoroughly until all ingredients are evenly blended together.

Note: calories may vary slightly due to brands and other recipe modifications.

Strawberry Espresso Surprise

Enjoy this rich textured and healthy strawberry espresso shake on that morning when you are looking for that extra fruity taste. You could substitute the cup of strawberry puree for a medium mashed banana or your favorite berries.

Makes: 1 Serving
Preparation Time: 5 Minutes
314 Calories per serving

Ingredients

- 1 cup (240ml) Skim Milk (or use your favorite dairy or non-dairy milk)
- ½ cup (120ml) unsweetened Strawberry Juice
- 1 scoop (28g) Vanilla Protein Powder
- ½ tablespoon (7.5ml) Organic Extra-virgin Coconut Oil or Coconut Butter
- 1 teaspoon (5g) Instant Ground Coffee
- 1 teaspoon (5g) unsweetened Cocoa Powder
- Natural Stevia or preferred sweetener to taste (optional)

Directions

Pour the milk, strawberry juice and protein powder in your blender bottle and shake well until the protein powder is completely dissolved.

Add the remaining ingredients to the protein powder mixture and shake thoroughly until all ingredients are evenly blended together.

Note: calories may vary slightly due to brands and other recipe modifications.

Mango Vanilla Peak

This morning shake represents nutritional comfort in its purest form. Pamper yourself with this stress buster while you enjoy this rich mango flavor in the morning. Just sip away and relax while you give your boost your vitamin and mineral levels.

Makes: *1 Serving*
Preparation Time: *5 Minutes*
318 Calories per serving

Ingredients

- 1 cup (240ml) Skim Milk (or use your favorite dairy or non-dairy milk)
- ½ cup (120ml) Mango Juice
- 1 scoop (28g) Vanilla Protein Powder
- 1 tablespoon (15g) Ground Chia Seeds (optional)
- 1 teaspoon (6ml) Vanilla Extract
- ¼ teaspoon (1g) Ground Nutmeg
- Pinch of Sea Salt

Directions

Pour the milk, mango juice and protein powder in your blender bottle and shake well until the protein powder is completely dissolved.

Add the remaining ingredients to the protein powder mixture and shake thoroughly until all ingredients are evenly blended together.

Note: calories may vary slightly due to brands and other recipe modifications.

Egg Nog Dream

Let's enjoy this delicious blend of rich morning protein. This shake combination pairs nicely with the pecan butter to make a perfect breakfast meal. Substituting the pecan butter for peanut butter is a worthwhile variation.

Makes: *1 Serving*
Preparation Time: *5 Minutes*
321 Calories per serving

Ingredients

- 1 cup (240ml) Skim Milk (or use your favorite dairy or non-dairy milk)
- 1 scoop (28g) Egg White Protein Powder
- 1 tablespoon (15g) Raw Pecan Butter
- 1 teaspoon (6ml) Vanilla Extract
- ¼ teaspoon (1g) Ground Nutmeg
- ½ teaspoon (2.5g) Cinnamon Powder
- Natural Stevia or preferred sweetener to taste
- Pinch of Sea Salt

Directions

Pour the milk and protein powder in your blender bottle and shake well until the protein powder is completely dissolved.

Add the remaining ingredients to the protein powder mixture and shake thoroughly until all ingredients are evenly blended together.

Note: calories may vary slightly due to brands and other recipe modifications.

Avocado Flax Pudding

The idea of putting avocado in your shake may seem weird at first, but this shake might surprise you. Give it a try and enjoy a healthy dose of Vitamin E and omega fatty acids.

Makes: *1 Serving*
Preparation Time: *10 Minutes*
391 Calories per serving

Ingredients

- ½ cup (120ml) Skim Milk (or use your favorite dairy or non-dairy milk)
- ¼ cup (60ml) unsweetened Strawberry Juice
- 1 scoop (28g) Vanilla Protein Powder
- 2 tablespoons (30g) Banana Flavor Pudding Mix
- ½ cup (120ml) Blueberry Yogurt
- 1 large slice (100g) of Ripe Avocado, mashed until creamy
- 1 tablespoon (15g) Ground Flaxseed

Directions

Pour the milk, strawberry juice, protein powder and banana pudding mix in your blender bottle and shake well until the protein powder is completely dissolved.

Add the remaining ingredients to the protein powder mixture and shake thoroughly until all ingredients are evenly blended together.

Note: calories may vary slightly due to brands and other recipe modifications.

Acai Berry Jello

Increasingly, acai berry is becoming widely known as a nutritious super food. Enjoy this acai berry shake which is combined with blueberry yogurt and chia seeds to give it that perfect nutritional balance of vitamins, fiber and protein.

Makes: *1 Serving*
Preparation Time: *10 Minutes*
410 Calories per serving

Ingredients

- 1 cup (240ml) unsweetened Acai Berry Juice
- 1 scoop (28g) Vanilla Protein Powder
- ½ cup (120ml) Strawberry Yogurt
- 1 tablespoon (15g) Ground Chia Seeds

Directions

Pour the acai berry juice and protein powder in your blender bottle and shake well until the protein powder is completely dissolved.

Add the remaining ingredients to the protein powder mixture and shake thoroughly until all ingredients are evenly blended together.

Note: calories may vary slightly due to brands and other recipe modifications.

Beta Goodness

Enjoy this healthy beta-carotene shake which is also complemented by the rich coconut milk flavor. This is a truly comforting mix that may uplift your dullest moment.

Makes: *1 Serving*
Preparation Time: *10 Minutes*
332 Calories per serving

Ingredients

- ¼ cup (60ml) Unsweetened Coconut Milk
- ¼ cup (60ml) unsweetened Carrot Juice
- ½ cup (120ml) unsweetened Mango Juice
- 1 scoop (28g) Vanilla Protein Powder
- ¼ teaspoon (1g) Ground Nutmeg
- Pinch of Sea Salt

Directions

Pour the coconut milk, carrot juice, mango juice and protein powder in your blender bottle and shake well until the protein powder is completely dissolved.

Add the remaining ingredients to the protein powder mixture and shake thoroughly until all ingredients are evenly blended together.

Note: calories may vary slightly due to brands and other recipe modifications.

Multi-Shake

This rich textured shake boasts exciting flavors of chocolate, strawberry, banana and vanilla. Enjoy every sip of this fulfilling and healthy shake and stay full for hours.

Makes: *1 Serving*
Preparation Time: *10 Minutes*
331.5 Calories per serving

Ingredients

- ¾ cup (180ml) Skim Milk (or use your favorite dairy or non-dairy milk)
- ¼ cup (60ml) unsweetened Strawberry Juice
- 1 scoop (28g) Vanilla Protein Powder
- 2 tablespoons (30g) Banana Flavor Pudding Mix
- 2 teaspoons (10g) unsweetened Cocoa Powder
- ½ teaspoon (2.5g) Cinnamon Powder

Directions

Pour the milk, strawberry juice and protein powder in your blender bottle and shake well until the protein powder is completely dissolved.

Add the remaining ingredients to the protein powder mixture and shake thoroughly until all ingredients are evenly blended together.

Note: calories may vary slightly due to brands and other recipe modifications.

Peachy Scotchie's

This beautiful peach flavored shake, with a delicious butterscotch twist, is truly fulfilling. You are guaranteed to enjoy this shake time and again, and you will feel more contented after each one.

Makes: *1 Serving*
Preparation Time: *10 Minutes*
370 Calories per serving

Ingredients

- 1 cup (240ml) Skim Milk (or use your favorite dairy or non-dairy milk)
- 1 scoop (28g) Protein Powder
- ½ cup (120ml) Peach Yogurt
- 2 tablespoons (30g) Butterscotch Pudding Mix

Directions

Pour the milk and protein powder in your blender bottle and shake well until the protein powder is completely dissolved.

Add the remaining ingredients to the protein powder mixture and shake thoroughly until all ingredients are evenly blended together.

Note: calories may vary slightly due to brands and other recipe modifications.

Avocado Power Medley

You can never go wrong with a creamy avocado shake that has a hint of citrus in the mix. Enjoy this slight gingery shake with essential fats, vitamins and protein to keep you going on a long day.

Makes: *1 Serving*
Preparation Time: *10 Minutes*
473.5 Calories per serving

Ingredients

- ½ cup (120ml) Skim Milk
- ½ cup (120ml) freshly squeezed Orange Juice
- 1 scoop (28g) Protein Powder
- 1 large slice (100g) of Ripe Avocado, mashed until creamy
- ½ of a Ripe Banana, mashed
- ½ teaspoon (2.5g) Ground Ginger

Directions

Pour the milk, orange juice and protein powder in your blender bottle and shake well until the protein powder is completely dissolved.

Add the remaining ingredients to the protein powder mixture and shake thoroughly until all ingredients are evenly blended together.

Note: calories may vary slightly due to brands and other recipe modifications.

Spiced Vanilla Blues

This shake is sure to please at just about any time you prefer. With a double-rich vanilla flavor with nutmeg spice in the mix, drinking this protein shake will be a pleasure.

Makes: *1 Serving*
Preparation Time: *10 Minutes*
313.5 Calories per serving

Ingredients

- ¾ cup (180ml) Skim Milk
- 1 scoop (28g) Vanilla Protein Powder
- ½ cup (120ml) Blueberry Yogurt
- 1 teaspoon (6ml) Vanilla Extract
- ½ teaspoon (2.5g) Ground Nutmeg

Directions

Pour the milk and protein powder in your blender bottle and shake well until the protein powder is completely dissolved.

Add the remaining ingredients to the protein powder mixture and shake thoroughly until all ingredients are evenly blended together.

Note: calories may vary slightly due to brands and other recipe modifications.

Go-Go Raspberry

By simply adding some raspberry juice to your shake, you'll be surprised at how good it will turn out. Whether you are a raspberry lover or not, give this shake a try and enjoy a rich vitamin boost as you also boost your protein intake.

Makes: *1 Serving*
Preparation Time: *10 Minutes*
261 Calories per serving

Ingredients

- 1 cup (240ml) Skim Milk
- 1 scoop (28g) Protein Powder
- ½ cup (120ml) Raspberry Nectar or Juice

Directions

Pour the milk and protein powder in your blender bottle and shake well until the protein powder is completely dissolved.

Add the remaining ingredient to the protein powder mixture and shake thoroughly until all ingredients are evenly blended together.

Note: calories may vary slightly due to brands and other recipe modifications.

Cran-Apple Berry

This shake nicely tones down the tarty cranberry taste and with apple juice. By adding the triple berry yogurt to this shake there is added protein benefits, plus a rich berry flavor.

Makes: *1 Serving*
Preparation Time: *10 Minutes*
278.5 Calories per serving

Ingredients

- ½ cup (120ml) Apple Juice
- ½ cup (120ml) Cranberry Juice
- 1 scoop (28g) Protein Powder
- ½ cup (120ml) Triple Berry Yogurt
- ½ teaspoon (2.5g) Ground Ginger

Directions

Pour the juices and protein powder in your blender bottle and shake well until the protein powder is completely dissolved.

Add the remaining ingredient to the protein powder mixture and shake thoroughly until all ingredients are evenly blended together.

Note: calories may vary slightly due to brands and other recipe modifications.

Rich Cherry Twist

Almonds and cherries pair well together in this fulfilling and healthy shake. With the added ground chia seeds you will also be unleashing the healthy benefits of this super food.

Makes: *1 Serving*
Preparation Time: *10 Minutes*
237 Calories per serving

Ingredients

- ¾ cup (180ml) unsweetened Almond Milk
- ½ cup unsweetened Cherry Juice
- 1 scoop (28g) Protein Powder
- Natural Stevia or preferred sweetener to taste
- 1 tablespoon (15g) Ground Chia Seeds

Directions

Pour the milk, cherry juice and protein powder in your blender bottle and shake well until the protein powder is completely dissolved.

Add the remaining ingredient to the protein powder mixture and shake thoroughly until all ingredients are evenly blended together.

Note: calories may vary slightly due to brands and other recipe modifications.

Pink Almond Pleasures

This shake uses the power of almonds to create a rich nutty taste with a pink base. Apart from strawberry juice, you may use cranberry juice for an entirely different taste while still enjoying a healthy protein shake.

Makes: *1 Serving*
Preparation Time: *10 Minutes*
324 Calories per serving

Ingredients

- ½ cup (180ml) Skim Milk (or use your favorite dairy or non-dairy milk)
- ½ cup (180ml) unsweetened Strawberry Juice (or Cranberry Juice)
- 1 scoop (28g) Protein Powder
- 1 tablespoon (15g) raw organic Almond Butter
- Natural Stevia or preferred sweetener to taste (optional)

Directions

Pour the milk, strawberry juice and protein powder in your blender bottle and shake well until the protein powder is completely dissolved.

Add the remaining ingredient to the protein powder mixture and shake thoroughly until all ingredients are evenly blended together.

Note: calories may vary slightly due to brands and other recipe modifications.

Citrus Detox Blend

If you feel like getting a detox, then this detoxifying shake would be your best pick. Harness the power of organic spinach powder with a nice citrus taste in the background. Lemons are great for detox purposes and will also help your body to alkalize for better health.

Makes: 1 Serving
Preparation Time: 10 Minutes
306 Calories per serving

Ingredients

- ¾ cup (180ml) unsweetened Organic Coconut Water
- ½ cup freshly squeezed Orange Juice
- 1 scoop (28g) Protein Powder
- 2 tablespoons (30g) raw organic Spinach Powder
- ½ teaspoon fresh Lemon Juice

Directions

Pour the coconut water, orange juice and powders in your blender bottle and shake well until the protein powder is completely dissolved.

Add the lemon juice to the protein powder mixture and shake thoroughly until all ingredients are evenly blended together.

Note: calories may vary slightly due to brands and other recipe modifications.

MUSCLE BUILDING PROTEIN SHAKES

Energy Medley

By including the power of the super food pomegranate, this shake nicely makes the perfect treat when you need some extra energy. So whether you want to drink this after you leave the gym or you want to drink this after some hard work, you'll surely be getting an energizing drink.

Makes: 1 Serving
Preparation Time: 10 Minutes
509 Calories per serving

Ingredients

- ½ cup (120ml) fresh unsweetened Pomegranate Juice
- ½ cup (120ml) unsweetened Almond Milk
- 2 scoops (56g) Protein Powder
- 1 tablespoon (15g) raw organic Nut Butter (pecan, almond or coconut)
- 1 large ripe Banana, mashed
- ¼ teaspoon (1g) Ground Ginger

Directions

Pour the pomegranate, almond milk and protein powder in your blender bottle and shake well until the protein powder is completely dissolved.

Add the remaining ingredients to the protein powder mixture and shake thoroughly until all ingredients are evenly blended together.

Note: calories may vary slightly due to brands and other recipe modifications.

Carrot Supreme

Carrots are used in this shake to deliver optimum nutritional benefits such as beta carotene, Vitamin A, C and E. This unique combination turns out to be quite creamy and will do well in replacing lost energy.

Makes: *1 Serving*
Preparation Time: *20 Minutes*
335 Calories per serving

Ingredients

- ½ cup (120ml) unsweetened Carrot Juice
- ½ cup (120ml) unsweetened Almond Milk
- 2 scoops (56g) Protein Powder
- ½ cup (120ml) low-fat vanilla Greek Yogurt
- Pinch of Sea Salt
- Stevia to taste (optional)

Directions

Pour the carrot juice, almond milk and protein powder in

your blender bottle and shake well until the protein powder is completely dissolved.

Add the remaining ingredients to the protein powder mixture and shake thoroughly until all ingredients are evenly blended together.

Note: calories may vary slightly due to brands and other recipe modifications.

Almond Power Frenzy

Enjoy this rich almond flavored shake which also happens to have a nice crunchy texture from the almond meal. There's nothing better than a healthy and energy giving shake after a hectic day or work-out.

Makes: 1 Serving
Preparation Time: 10 Minutes
551 Calories per serving

Ingredients

- ¾ cup (180ml) unsweetened Almond Milk
- 2 scoops (56g) Protein Powder
- 1 tablespoon (15g) raw organic Almond Butter
- *¼ cup (38g) Almond Meal
- ½ cup (120ml) low-fat vanilla Greek Yogurt
- ½ teaspoon (2.5g) Cinnamon Powder

Directions

Pour the almond milk and protein powder in your blender bottle and shake well until the protein powder is completely dissolved.

Add the remaining ingredients to the protein powder mixture and shake thoroughly until all ingredients are evenly blended together.

Note: calories may vary slightly due to brands and other recipe modifications.

Pecan Vanilla Cream

Enjoy the added fiber and flavor from this pecan vanilla shake. It is protein packed and offers a really rich and creamy texture. This shake is also loaded with healthy fats that work well with the protein to boost energy levels.

Makes: *1 Serving*
Preparation Time: *10 Minutes*
617 Calories per serving

Ingredients

- 1 cup (240ml) fat-free Milk
- 2 scoops (56g) Protein Powder
- ½ cup (120ml) low-fat vanilla Greek Yogurt
- ¼ cup (38g) Pecan Meal
- 1 teaspoon (6ml) Vanilla Extract
- 1 tablespoon (15g) Natural Stevia or preferred sweetener to taste
- Pinch of Sea Salt
- 1 scoop (28g) Protein Powder

Directions

Pour the milk and protein powder in your blender bottle and shake well until the protein powder is completely dissolved.

Add the remaining ingredients to the protein powder mixture and shake thoroughly until all ingredients are evenly blended together.

Note: calories may vary slightly due to brands and other recipe modifications.

Go-Large Berry Fix

Sometimes keeping your shake simple can offer great health benefits as well. This shake is made of simple ingredients, but also offers the benefits of rich protein mingled with omega fatty acids. Enjoy every sip.

Makes: *1 Serving*
Preparation Time: *10 Minutes*
562 Calories per serving

Ingredients

- ½ cup (120ml) Skim Milk (or use your favorite dairy or non-dairy milk)
- 2 scoops (56g) Protein Powder
- 1 cup (240ml) Triple Berry Yogurt, low fat
- 1 tablespoon Flaxseed Oil

Directions

Pour the milk and protein powder in your blender bottle and shake well until the protein powder is completely dissolved.

Add the remaining ingredients to the protein powder

mixture and shake thoroughly until all ingredients are evenly blended together.

Note: calories may vary slightly due to brands and other recipe modifications.

Choco-bana Special

A delicious recipe for your chocolate flavored protein powder and it offers the great energy benefits whenever you need it most. Be free to make your preferred milk substitute and still end up with an energy packed protein drink.

Makes: 1 Serving
Preparation Time: 10 Minutes
514 Calories per serving

Ingredients

- 1 cup (240ml) fat-free Milk (or use your favorite dairy or non-dairy milk)
- 2 scoops (56g) Chocolate Protein Powder
- 1 large ripe Banana, mashed
- 1 tablespoon Acai Powder
- 1 teaspoon (6ml) Vanilla Extract
- Natural Stevia or preferred sweetener to taste
- Pinch of Sea Salt

Directions

Pour the milk and protein powder in your blender bottle and shake well until the protein powder is completely dissolved. Add the remaining ingredients to the protein powder

mixture and shake thoroughly until all ingredients are evenly blended together.

Note: calories may vary slightly due to brands and other recipe modifications.

Cheese Wiz Shake

Help build up your muscle power with this great tasting cheese shake. The vitamin boost of milk, cheese and flax oil will leave you feeling ready to tackle any set of weights you see in the gym.

Makes: 1 Serving
Preparation Time: 5 Minutes
484 Calories per serving

Ingredients

- 1 cup (240ml) Fat-Free Milk
- 2 scoops (56g) Vanilla Protein Powder
- ½ cup (120ml) Low-fat Cottage Cheese
- 1 teaspoon (6ml) Flax Oil

Directions

Pour the milk and protein powder in your blender bottle and shake well until the protein powder is completely dissolved.

Add the remaining ingredients and shake thoroughly until all ingredients are evenly blended together.

Note: calories may vary slightly due to brands and other recipe modifications.

Coconut Twister Shake

If you love the sweet taste of coconut, you'll love this shake! The coconut is complemented beautifully with the strawberry nectar to provide a great tasting base to this power boosting drink.

Makes: *1 Serving*
Preparation Time: *5 Minutes*
651.5 Calories per serving

Ingredients
- ½ cup (120ml) Organic Unsweetened Coconut Milk
- 2 scoops (56g) Protein Powder
- ¾ cup (180ml) Strawberry Nectar or Juice
- ½ of a large Banana, mashed

Directions
Pour the coconut milk and protein powder in your blender bottle and shake well until the protein powder is completely dissolved.

Add the remaining ingredients and shake thoroughly until all ingredients are evenly blended together.

Note: calories may vary slightly due to brands and other recipe modifications.

Peach Cobbler Shake

A double boost of protein powder, combined with a cup of milk and peach juice creates a perfect shake to boost your muscle building workout. The addition of maple syrup in this recipe gives a great sweet kick to this delicious shake.

Makes: *1 Serving*
Preparation Time: *5 Minutes*
403 Calories per serving

Ingredients

- 1 cup (240ml) Skim Milk
- 2 scoops (56g) Protein Powder
- ½ cup (120ml) unsweetened Peach Juice
- 1 teaspoon (6ml) Maple Syrup

Directions

Pour the milk and protein powder in your blender bottle and shake well until the protein powder is completely dissolved.

Add the remaining ingredients and shake thoroughly until all ingredients are evenly blended together.

Note: calories may vary slightly due to brands and other recipe modifications.

Mango Tango Shake

The fruit juice infusion in this shake, not only adds a wonderful variety of vitamins, but is also gives this shake a tropical taste. Picture yourself on a Caribbean beach after drinking this shake whilst you develop your muscles!

Makes: *1 Serving*
Preparation Time: *5 Minutes*
407 Calories per serving

Ingredients

- ½ cup Unsweetened Mango Juice
- ½ cup Unsweetened Pineapple Juice
- ½ cup (240ml) Orange Juice
- 2 scoops (56g) Protein Powder

Directions

Add all the ingredients in the blender bottle and shake well until all ingredients are evenly blended together.

Note: calories may vary slightly due to brands and other recipe modifications.

Orange Cream Sickle Shake

The mixture of orange juice and banana cream pie yogurt provides a great tasting and creamy shake. The addition of ground chia seeds adds a healthy kick and rich fiber to this shake.

Makes: *1 Serving*
Preparation Time: *5 Minutes*
421 Calories per serving

Ingredients

- 1 cup (240ml) Orange Juice
- 2 scoops (56g) Vanilla Protein Powder
- ½ cup (120ml) Banana Cream Pie Yogurt
- 2 tablespoons (30g) Ground Chia Seed

Directions

Pour the orange juice and protein powder in your blender bottle and shake well until the protein powder is completely dissolved.

Add the remaining ingredients and shake thoroughly until all ingredients are evenly blended together.

Note: calories may vary slightly due to brands and other recipe modifications.

Creamy Chocolate Caramel Shake

For lovers of chocolate, this shake will give you great taste of hot chocolate, but packed in a wonderfully tasting milk based shake. The added nutrients provided by the hemp powder will make you feel great while you pump some iron.

Makes: 1 Serving
Preparation Time: 5 Minutes
300 Calories per serving

Ingredients

- 1 cup (240ml) Unsweetened Almond Milk
- 2 scoops (56g) Chocolate Protein Powder
- 1 teaspoon (5g) Hemp Powder

- 1 teaspoon (5g) Caramel Creamer

Directions

Pour the milk and protein powder in your blender bottle and shake well until the protein powder is completely dissolved.

Add the remaining ingredients and shake thoroughly until all ingredients are evenly blended together.

Note: calories may vary slightly due to brands and other recipe modifications.

Almond Pineapple Shake

The calcium and iron boost provided by the almond milk and butter in this shake will help you to feel energized after having a good work out at the gym. The addition of pineapple juice adds a lovely sweetness to this great tasting shake.

Makes: 1 Serving
Preparation Time: 5 Minutes
437 Calories per serving

Ingredients

- ½ cup (120ml) Almond Milk
- ¾ cup (180ml) unsweetened Pineapple Juice
- 2 Scoops (56g) Protein Powder
- 1 tablespoon (15g) raw Almond Butter

Directions

Pour the milk, pineapple juice and protein powder in your blender bottle and shake well until the protein powder is completely dissolved.

Add the remaining ingredients and shake thoroughly until all ingredients are evenly blended together.

Note: calories may vary slightly due to brands and other recipe modifications.

Cinnamon Chocolate Dream Shake

As the name suggests, this really is a dream shake! A double boost of chocolate protein powder combined with almond milk, banana and chia seeds not only tastes great, but this shake is packed with vitamins and rich nutrients.

Makes: 1 Serving
Preparation Time: 5 Minutes
350.5 Calories per serving

Ingredients

- 1 cup (240ml) unsweetened Almond Milk
- 2 scoops (56g) Chocolate Protein Powder
- ½ of a large Banana, mashed
- 1 teaspoon (5g) Cinnamon Powder
- 2 tablespoon (30g) Ground Chia Seed

Directions

Pour the milk and protein powder in your blender bottle and shake well until the protein powder is completely dissolved.

Add the remaining ingredients and shake thoroughly until all ingredients are evenly blended together.

Note: calories may vary slightly due to brands and other recipe modifications.

Peanut Butter Banana Shake

Peanut butter lovers will drink this shake time and again. The creaminess of the peanut butter, coupled with the banana adds a great texture to this drink. The use of vanilla protein powder also combines to give this shake a great flavor.

Makes: 1 Serving
Preparation Time: 5 Minutes
586.5 Calories per serving

Ingredients

- 1 cup (240ml) Skim Milk
- 2 scoops (56g) Vanilla Protein Powder
- 2 tablespoons (30g) Peanut Butter
- ½ of a large Banana, mashed

Directions

Pour the milk and protein powder in your blender bottle and shake well until the protein powder is completely dissolved.

Add the remaining ingredients and shake thoroughly until all ingredients are evenly blended together.

Note: calories may vary slightly due to brands and other recipe modifications.

Coco-Strawberry Shake

This shake has a lovely delicate strawberry, chocolate and coconut combination taste. It is a great pre-workout boost.

Makes: *1 Serving*
Preparation Time: *5 Minutes*
428 Calories per serving

Ingredients

- 1 cup (240ml) Soy Milk
- 2 scoops (56g) Chocolate Whey Protein Powder
- ½ cup (120ml) fat-free Strawberry Yogurt
- 1 tablespoon (15g) Coconut Butter

Directions

Pour the milk and protein powder in your blender bottle and shake well until the protein powder is completely dissolved.

Add the remaining ingredients and shake thoroughly until all ingredients are evenly blended together.

Note: calories may vary slightly due to brands and other recipe modifications.

Coffee Pleaser Shake

For coffee lovers, this is the perfect shake for anytime of the day. The energy boosting benefits of this drink will also help to provide extra stamina after you have finished your daily workout routine.

Makes: 1 Serving
Preparation Time: 5 Minutes
393 Calories per serving

Ingredients

- 1 cup (240ml) brewed Coffee, cooled and chilled
- 2 scoops (56g) Protein Powder
- ½ cup (240ml) Vanilla Yogurt
- 1 tablespoon (15ml) Honey

Directions

Pour the coffee and protein powder in your blender bottle and shake well until the protein powder is completely dissolved.

Add the remaining ingredients and shake thoroughly until all ingredients are evenly blended together.

Note: calories may vary slightly due to brands and other recipe modifications.

Citrus Pecan Shake

This shake, not only tastes great, but with the addition of pecan meal you will benefit from the antioxidants and rich fiber that this ingredient brings to this drink. This shake will help you stay healthy while you work at building your muscles.

Makes: *1 Serving*
Preparation Time: *5 Minutes*
643 Calories per serving

Ingredients

- ½ cup (120ml) Skim Milk
- ½ cup (120ml) Orange Juice
- 2 scoops (56g) Vanilla Protein Powder
- ½ cup (120ml) Key Lime Yogurt
- ¼ cup (38g) Pecan Meal

Directions

Pour the milk, orange juice and protein powder in your blender bottle and shake well until the protein powder is completely dissolved.

Add the remaining ingredients and shake thoroughly until all ingredients are evenly blended together.

Note: calories may vary slightly due to brands and other recipe modifications.

Whipped Chocolate Shake

This creamy and chocolaty shake is bursting with nutritional goodness. It is tasty pre- or post-workout energy booster and will be a hit for the gym.

Makes: *1 Serving*
Preparation Time: *5 Minutes*
662 Calories per serving

Ingredients

- 1 cup (240ml) Soy Milk
- 2 scoops (56g) Chocolate Protein Powder
- 2 tablespoons (30g) Whipping Cream
- 1 tablespoon (15g) Almond Butter
- 1 tablespoon (15ml) Flax Oil

Directions

Pour the milk and protein powder in your blender bottle and shake well until the protein powder is completely dissolved.

Add the remaining ingredients and shake thoroughly until all ingredients are evenly blended together.

Note: calories may vary slightly due to brands and other recipe modifications.

Mixed Fruit Shake

This fruity delight will provide a great energy boost before any physical workout. The combination of the fruit juices, powdered wheat grass and the protein powder provides nutrients, proteins and loads of energy.

Makes: 1 Serving
Preparation Time: 5 Minutes
497 Calories per serving

Ingredients

- ½ cup (120ml) unsweetened Apple

Juice
- 2 scoops (56g) Protein Powder
- ½ cup (120ml) Strawberry Nectar
- ½ cup (120ml) Kiwi Sauce
- 1 teaspoon (5g) Powdered Wheat Grass

Directions

Pour the apple juice and protein powder in your blender bottle and shake well until the protein powder is completely dissolved.

Add the remaining ingredients and shake thoroughly until all ingredients are evenly blended together.

Note: calories may vary slightly due to brands and other recipe modifications.

Mocha Hazelnut Delight Shake

The combination of coffee, cream and hazelnuts will have you relaxed and believing you are in your favorite a coffee house. The energy boost this shake provides will help you to recover from your workout and be ready to face the world again.

Makes: 1 Serving
Preparation Time: 5 Minutes
284 Calories per serving

Ingredients
- ½ cup (120ml) brewed Coffee, cooled

and chilled
- ½ cup Unsweetened Almond Milk
- 2 scoops (56g) Protein Powder
- 1 teaspoon (5g) Caramel Creamer
- 2 teaspoons (10ml) Hazelnut Extract

Directions

Pour the coffee, milk and protein powder in your blender bottle and shake well until the protein powder is completely dissolved.

Add the remaining ingredients and shake thoroughly until all ingredients are evenly blended together.

Note: calories may vary slightly due to brands and other recipe modifications.

PROTEIN SHAKES FOR WEIGHT LOSS

Banana Cinnamon Shake

The presence of banana in this shake provides a good source of nutrients, vitamins and minerals, as well as fiber. This great tasting shake has a lovely texture from the use of peanut butter, will help you maintain a healthy diet and will stop you feeling hungry between meals.

Makes: 1 Serving
Preparation Time: 5 Minutes
378 Calories per serving

Ingredients

- 1 cup (240ml) Fat-free Milk
- 1 scoop (28g) Protein Powder
- ½ of a large Banana, mashed
- 1 tablespoon (15g) Reduced-fat Peanut Butter
- 1 teaspoon (15ml) Vanilla Extract
- Pinch of Ground Cinnamon

Directions

Pour the milk and protein powder in your blender bottle and shake well until the protein powder is completely dissolved.

Add the remaining ingredients to the protein powder mixture and shake thoroughly until all ingredients are evenly blended together.

Note: calories may vary slightly due to brands and other recipe modifications.

Blueberry Flax Shake

Blueberries are one of the obvious ingredients in many weight loss recipes because of their high content level of antioxidants. This recipe will be a great addition to your diet and in the end you will have healthy and tasty shake.

Makes: 1 Serving
Preparation Time: 5 Minutes
423 Calories per serving

Ingredients

- 1 cup (240ml) unsweetened Blueberry Juice
- 1 scoop (28g) Protein Powder
- ½ of a large Banana, mashed
- ½ tablespoon (8ml) Flaxseed Oil
- 1 tablespoon (15g) Ground Flaxseed

Directions

Pour the blueberry juice and protein powder in your blender

bottle and shake well until the protein powder is completely dissolved.

Add the remaining ingredients to the protein powder mixture and shake thoroughly until all ingredients are evenly blended together.

Note: calories may vary slightly due to brands and other recipe modifications.

Mocha Vanilla Shake

Want a coffee flavored shake? This shake will hit the spot whenever you are craving for a coffee fix. This shake may even become a firm favorite for coffee breaks at work.

Makes: 1 *Serving*
Preparation Time: 5 *Minutes*
202 Calories per serving

Ingredients
- ½ cup (120ml) Fat-free Milk
- 1 scoop (28g) Chocolate Protein Powder
- 1 cup (240ml) fat-free Vanilla Yogurt
- 1 teaspoon (5g) Instant Ground Coffee
- 2 teaspoon (5g) unsweetened Cocoa Powder

Directions
Pour the milk and protein powder in your blender bottle and shake well until the protein powder is completely dissolved.

Add the remaining ingredients to the protein powder mixture and shake thoroughly until all ingredients are evenly

blended together.

Note: calories may vary slightly due to brands and other recipe modifications.

Slimming Berry Shake

This great tasting shake combines the exotic taste of raspberries with a delicious low-fat strawberry yogurt. The vanilla and nutmeg touch will give this drink a subtle aftertaste which you'll love. Enjoy every sip of this shake and the interesting raspberry weight loss benefits.

Makes: 1 Serving
Preparation Time: 5 Minutes
335 Calories per serving

Ingredients
- 1 cup (240ml) unsweetened Raspberry Juice
- 1 scoop (28g) Vanilla Protein Powder
- ½ cup (120ml) Fat-free Strawberry Yogurt
- 1 teaspoon (6ml) Vanilla Extract
- ¼ teaspoon (1g) Ground Nutmeg

Directions
Pour the raspberry juice and protein powder in your blender bottle and shake well until the protein powder is completely dissolved.

Add the remaining ingredients to the protein powder mixture and shake thoroughly until all ingredients are evenly

blended together.

Note: calories may vary slightly due to brands and other recipe modifications.

Sentimental Strawberry Shake

This low calorie shake not only tastes and looks great, it will satisfy your hunger pangs immediately. This shake will become a good addition to your new and healthy way of eating.

Makes: *1 Serving*
Preparation Time: *5 Minutes*
222 Calories per serving

Ingredients

- ½ cup (120ml) Fat-free Milk
- ½ cup (120ml) Water
- 1 scoop (28g) Vanilla Protein Powder
- ¼ cup (60ml) Strawberry Nectar
- 1 teaspoon (6ml) Banana Extract
- ¼ teaspoon (1g) Ground Cinnamon

Directions

Pour the milk, water and protein powder in your blender bottle and shake well until the protein powder is completely dissolved.

Add the remaining ingredients to the protein powder mixture and shake thoroughly until all ingredients are evenly blended together.

Note: calories may vary slightly due to brands and other recipe modifications.

Berry Granola Shake

Who can resist the delicious taste of mixed berries? This shake has an inviting red color which will make you want to have this time and again. The addition of granola gives this shake a great source of fiber and a wonderful texture. This shake is a great way to start the day.

Makes: 1 Serving
Preparation Time: 5 Minutes
336 Calories per serving

Ingredients

- 1 cup (240ml) unsweetened Mixed Berry Juice
- 1 scoop (28g) Protein Powder
- ¼ teaspoon (1g) Ground Nutmeg
- ¼ cup (38g) Low-fat Granola
- Natural Stevia (or sweetener of your choice) to taste

Directions

Pour the mixed berry juice and protein powder in your blender bottle and shake well until the protein powder is completely dissolved.

Add the remaining ingredients to the protein powder mixture and shake thoroughly until all ingredients are evenly blended together.

Note: calories may vary slightly due to brands and other recipe modifications.

Kiwi Apple Shake

This refreshing shake combines the wonderful tastes of apple and kiwi. You will enjoy making this shake any time of day and you will feel refreshed after every sip.

Makes: *1 Serving*
Preparation Time: *5 Minutes*
340 Calories per serving

Ingredients

- 1 cup (240ml) unsweetened Apple Juice
- 1 scoop (28g) Protein Powder
- ½ cup (120ml) Kiwi Sauce
- 1 teaspoon (6g) Lemon Juice

Directions

Pour the apple juice and protein powder in your blender bottle and shake well until the protein powder is completely dissolved.

Add the remaining ingredients to the protein powder mixture and shake thoroughly until all ingredients are evenly blended together.

Note: calories may vary slightly due to brands and other recipe modifications.

Cranberry Almond Shake

The health benefits of almond and cranberry are abundant in this great tasting shake. You can relax and enjoy this drink while you are also loading your body with healthy vitamins and antioxidants.

Makes: *1 Serving*

Preparation Time: 5 Minutes
288 Calories per serving

Ingredients
- 1 cup (240ml) Almond Milk
- 1 scoop (28g) Protein Powder
- ½ cup (120ml) unsweetened Cranberry Juice
- 1 tablespoon (15g) raw Almond Butter

Directions
Pour the almond milk and protein powder in your blender bottle and shake well until the protein powder is completely dissolved.

Add the remaining ingredients to the protein powder mixture and shake thoroughly until all ingredients are evenly blended together.

Note: calories may vary slightly due to brands and other recipe modifications.

Avocado Lemon Pie Shake
Avocado is a great fruit packed with Omega 9 fatty acid and is perfect for your diet as this fruit will speed up the conversion of fat into energy, and it will also increase your metabolic rate. Enjoy this healthy and delicious shake as often as you want to.

Makes: 1 Serving
Preparation Time: 5 Minutes

407 Calories per serving

Ingredients

- ¾ cup (180ml) Water
- 1 scoop (28g) Protein Powder
- ½ tablespoon (7.5ml) Lemon Juice
- ½ cup (120ml) Fat-free Lemon Yogurt
- 1 large slice (100g) of Ripe Avocado, mashed until creamy
- 1 tablespoon (15g) Stevia

Directions

Pour the water and protein powder in your blender bottle and shake well until the protein powder is completely dissolved.

Add the remaining ingredients to the protein powder mixture and shake thoroughly until all ingredients are evenly blended together.

Note: calories may vary slightly due to brands and other recipe modifications.

Coconut Vanilla Shake

This shake is a perfect drink for all coconut lovers. As well as, with coconut water being low in fat, it also helps you to feel full, thus reducing the desire to snack between meals. Enjoy this shake at any time of the day.

Makes: 1 Serving
Preparation Time: 5 Minutes
326 Calories per serving

Ingredients

- ½ cup (120ml) unsweetened Organic Coconut Water
- 1 scoop (28g) Vanilla Protein Powder
- 1 cup (240ml) Fat-free Vanilla Yogurt
- 1 tablespoon (15g) Coconut Extract
- ¼ teaspoon (1g) Ground Nutmeg

Directions

Pour the coconut water and protein powder in your blender bottle and shake well until the protein powder is completely dissolved.

Add the remaining ingredients to the protein powder mixture and shake thoroughly until all ingredients are evenly blended together.

Note: calories may vary slightly due to brands and other recipe modifications.

Peachy Bliss Shake

As the name suggests, this peach shake is truly delicious. The addition of yogurt in this shake will aid weight loss as your body's ability to burn up fat is increased with more calcium into your diet. This shake will become a favorite pick-me-up when life feels stressful.

Makes: 1 Serving
Preparation Time: 5 Minutes
330 Calories per serving

Ingredients

- ½ cup (120ml) unsweetened Peach Juice
- 1 scoop (28g) Protein Powder
- 1 cup (240ml) Fat-free Peach Yogurt
- 1 teaspoon (5ml) Flaxseed Oil

Directions

Pour the peach juice and protein powder in your blender bottle and shake well until the protein powder is completely dissolved.

Add the remaining ingredients to the protein powder mixture and shake thoroughly until all ingredients are evenly blended together.

Note: calories may vary slightly due to brands and other recipe modifications.

Orange Vanilla Shake

The combination of lemon yogurt with orange creates a great citrus taste to this shake. This shake will revitalize you after a hard day and will help you to feel refreshed to tackle whatever is thrown your way.

Makes: 1 Serving
Preparation Time: 5 Minutes
317 Calories per serving

Ingredients

- ½ cup (120ml) Water
- 1 scoop (28g) Vanilla Protein Powder

- ½ cup (120ml) Fat-free Lemon Yogurt
- ½ cup (120ml) Orange Juice
- 1 teaspoon (5ml) Virgin Organic Coconut Oil

Directions

Pour the water and protein powder in your blender bottle and shake well until the protein powder is completely dissolved.

Add the remaining ingredients to the protein powder mixture and shake thoroughly until all ingredients are evenly blended together.

Note: calories may vary slightly due to brands and other recipe modifications.

Apple Pie Shake

If you love apple pie but can't have it whilst on your diet, then this shake is for you. The combination of apple juice, unsweetened applesauce and apple pie spice creates the next best thing to a freshly baked apple pie. Indulge yourself with this shake safe in the knowledge that you'll be losing weight rather than putting it on!

Makes: 1 Serving
Preparation Time: 5 Minutes
344 Calories per serving

Ingredients

- ½ cup (120ml) Fat-free Milk
- ½ cup (120ml) unsweetened Apple Juice
- 1 scoop (28g) Protein Powder

- 2 tablespoons unsweetened Applesauce
- 1 teaspoon (5g) Apple Pie Spice
- 1 tablespoon (15g) Nut Butter

Directions

Pour the milk, apple juice and protein powder in your blender bottle and shake well until the protein powder is completely dissolved.

Add the remaining ingredients to the protein powder mixture and shake thoroughly until all ingredients are evenly blended together.

Note: calories may vary slightly due to brands and other recipe modifications.

Pineapple Flax Shake

Flaxseeds are known to be a good source of healthy fats and fiber. It is a great ingredient in this shake as it will help you to feel full and not to be tempted to sneak a naught treat between meals. Plan to have this shake when you know you will be tempted and you'll reap the full benefits.

Makes: 1 Serving
Preparation Time: 5 Minutes
335 Calories per serving

Ingredients

- 1 cup (240) unsweetened Pineapple Juice
- ½ cup (120ml) Fat-free Milk
- 1 scoop (28g) Protein Powder
- 1 tablespoon (15g) Ground Flaxseed

Directions

Pour the pineapple juice and protein powder in your blender bottle and shake well until the protein powder is completely dissolved.

Add the remaining ingredients to the protein powder mixture and shake thoroughly until all ingredients are evenly blended together.

Note: calories may vary slightly due to brands and other recipe modifications.

Raspberry Avocado Shake

This simple shake has four ingredients, yet it makes a great tasting, creamy drink. This delicious drink is ideal to make whenever you are pressed for time.

Makes: *1 Serving*
Preparation Time: *5 Minutes*
426 Calories per serving

Ingredients

- 1 cup (240ml) unsweetened Raspberry Juice
- 1 scoop (28g) Vanilla Protein Powder
- 1 large slice (100g) of Ripe Avocado, mashed until creamy
- ¼ cup (60ml) Water

Directions

Pour the raspberry juice and protein powder in your blender bottle and shake well until the protein powder is completely dissolved.

Add the remaining ingredients to the protein powder mixture and shake thoroughly until all ingredients are evenly blended together.

Note: calories may vary slightly due to brands and other recipe modifications.

Silken Banana Cocoa Shake

Tofu, an excellent source of proteins and calcium, is often regarded as bland food for hippies. Shake off these preconceptions and enjoy this versatile ingredient in this fantastically delicious shake. Once you've tasted this drink you're likely to become hooked.

Makes: 1 Serving
Preparation Time: 5 Minutes
243 Calories per serving

Ingredients

- ½ cup (120ml) Fat-free Milk
- 1 scoop (28g) Chocolate Protein Powder
- ½ of a large Banana, mashed
- ½ cup (120ml) Silken Tofu
- 1 tablespoon (15g) unsweetened Cocoa Powder
- Stevia to taste

Directions

Pour the milk and protein powder in your blender bottle and shake well until the protein powder is completely dissolved.

Add the remaining ingredients to the protein powder mixture and shake thoroughly until all ingredients are evenly blended together.

Note: calories may vary slightly due to brands and other recipe modifications.

Fruity Vanilla Dream Shake

This shake, having a mixture of blueberry, vanilla and peach, is a delight to drink at any time of the day. You will not only enjoy the flavors of this shake, but you'll also enjoy knowing that this drink is boosting your vitamin and protein levels at the same time.

Makes: *1 Serving*
Preparation Time: *5 Minutes*
256.5 Calories per serving

Ingredients

- ½ cup (120ml) unsweetened Blueberry Juice
- ½ cup (120ml) Water
- 1 scoop (28g) Vanilla Protein Powder
- ½ cup (120ml) fat-free Peach Yogurt
- 1 teaspoon (5ml) Vanilla Extract

Directions

Pour the blueberry juice and protein powder in your blender bottle and shake well until the protein powder is completely dissolved.

Add the remaining ingredients to the protein powder mixture and shake thoroughly until all ingredients are evenly blended together.

Note: calories may vary slightly due to brands and other recipe modifications.

Tangy Berry Spinach Shake

When you want to have a shake that excites your taste buds, as well as giving you a health kick and being low in calories, this is the one! Each time you have this shake you'll enjoy the tangy taste as though it is the first time you have tried this.

Makes: *1 Serving*
Preparation Time: *5 Minutes*
285.5 Calories per serving

Ingredients

- ½ cup (120ml) unsweetened Raspberry Juice
- ½ cup (120ml) unsweetened Orange Juice
- 1 scoop (28g) Protein Powder
- ¼ cup Fat-free Strawberry Yogurt
- 1 tablespoon (15g) Organic Spinach Powder

Directions

Pour the raspberry juice and protein powder in your blender bottle and shake well until the protein powder is completely dissolved.

Add the remaining ingredients to the protein powder mixture and shake thoroughly until all ingredients are evenly blended together.

Note: calories may vary slightly due to brands and other recipe modifications.

Almond Joy Shake

As the name suggests, this shake is rich in almond flavors. If you are not a fan of almond nuts, you will be pleasantly surprised by the delicious taste of this drink. Everyone who has this drink will also benefit greatly from the fantastic health benefits provided by the almond milk, butter and meal.

Makes: 1 *Serving*
Preparation Time: 5 *Minutes*
374 Calories per serving

Ingredients

- 1 cup (240ml) unsweetened Almond Milk
- 1 scoop (28g) Protein Powder
- ½ tablespoon (8g) raw Almond Butter
- ¼ cup (38g) Almond Meal
- ½ teaspoon (2.5g) Coconut Extract

Directions

Pour the milk and protein powder in your blender bottle and shake well until the protein powder is completely dissolved.

Add the remaining ingredients to the protein powder mixture and shake thoroughly until all ingredients are evenly blended together.

Note: calories may vary slightly due to brands and other recipe modifications.

Fruit Medley Shake

The exotic flavors of banana and pineapple combine beautifully with the strawberry nectar in this recipe. Enjoy this shake and the amazing health benefits.

Makes: 1 Serving
Preparation Time: 5 Minutes
348 Calories per serving

Ingredients

- ½ cup (120ml) Fat-free Milk
- ½ cup (120ml) unsweetened Pineapple Juice
- 1 Scoop (28g) Vanilla Protein Powder
- ¼ cup (60ml) Strawberry Nectar
- 1 teaspoon (6ml) Banana Extract
- ½ of a large Banana, mashed

Directions

Pour the milk, pineapple juice and protein powder in your blender bottle and shake well until the protein powder is completely dissolved.

Add the remaining ingredients to the protein powder mixture and shake thoroughly until all ingredients are evenly blended together.

Note: calories may vary slightly due to brands and other recipe modifications.

LOW SUGAR & LOW CARB SHAKES

Almond Twist Shake

This almond twist shake combines blueberry juice with yogurt, almond meal and wheat germ. This shake is a great way to start your day and will leave you energized and fulfilled.

Makes: *1 Serving*
Preparation Time: *5 Minutes*
501 Calories per serving

Ingredients
- 1 cup (240ml) unsweetened Blueberry Juice
- 1 scoop (28g) Sugar-free Protein Powder
- ½ cup (120ml) Fat-free Plain Greek Yogurt
- ¼ cup (38g) Almond Meal
- 2 tablespoons (30g) Wheat Germ

Directions
Pour the juice and protein powder in your blender bottle and shake well until the protein powder is completely dissolved. Add the remaining ingredients to the protein powder

mixture and shake thoroughly until all ingredients are evenly blended together.

Note: calories may vary slightly due to brands and other recipe modifications.

Raspberry Butter Swirl Shake

Peanut butter, being rich in unsaturated fat and protein, is a great addition to any shake for diabetics. This delicious drink, with a lovely crunchy texture, will leave you wanting more.

Makes: *1 Serving*
Preparation Time: *5 Minutes*
441 Calories per serving

Ingredients

- 1 cup (240ml) unsweetened Raspberry Juice
- 1 scoop (28g) Sugar-free Protein Powder
- 2 tablespoons (30ml) Skim Milk (or preferred milk of choice)
- 2 tablespoons (30g) raw natural Peanut Butter

Directions

Pour the raspberry juice and protein powder in your blender bottle and shake well until the protein powder is completely dissolved.

Add the remaining ingredients to the protein powder

mixture and shake thoroughly until all ingredients are evenly blended together.

Note: calories may vary slightly due to brands and other recipe modifications.

Strawberry Flax Shake

This shake is a great way to add avocado into your diet without having to worry about your blood sugar levels. The combination of avocado with strawberry juice, milk and ground flax seed means the carbohydrate levels in this shake are low. Enjoy this creamy, fruity tasting drink anytime of the day.

Makes: 1 Serving
Preparation Time: 5 Minutes
515 Calories per serving

Ingredients

- 1 cup (240ml) unsweetened Strawberry Juice
- 2 tablespoons (15ml) Skim Milk (or preferred milk of choice)
- 1 scoop (28g) Sugar-free Protein Powder
- 1 large slice (100g) of Ripe Avocado, mashed until creamy
- 2 tablespoons (30g) Ground Flax Seed

Directions

Pour the strawberry juice, milk and protein powder in your blender bottle and shake well until the protein powder is completely dissolved.

Add the remaining ingredients to the protein powder mixture and shake thoroughly until all ingredients are evenly blended together.

Note: calories may vary slightly due to brands and other recipe modifications.

Apple Spinach Shake

Flax seed has been linked with reducing blood sugar levels after a meal, so this shake is a great way to introduce this ingredient into your diet. Relax and enjoy this great tasting shake after a meal, or have it as a delicious and healthy dessert.

Makes: *1 Serving*
Preparation Time: *5 Minutes*
395 Calories per serving

Ingredients

- 1 cup (240ml) unsweetened Apple Juice
- 1 scoop (28g) Sugar-free Protein Powder
- ½ cup (120ml) Fat-free Greek Yogurt
- 2 tablespoons (30g) Organic Spinach Powder
- 2 tablespoons (30g) Flax Seed Meal

Directions

Pour the apple juice and protein powder in your blender

bottle and shake well until the protein powder is completely dissolved.

Add the remaining ingredients to the protein powder mixture and shake thoroughly until all ingredients are evenly blended together.

Note: calories may vary slightly due to brands and other recipe modifications.

Raspberry Cinnamon Shake

Berries are believed to be a super food for diabetics as they are loaded with antioxidants, fiber and vitamins. Indulge yourself with this great tasting shake which is perfect anytime of the day.

Makes: *1 Serving*
Preparation Time: *5 Minutes*
298 Calories per serving

Ingredients
- 1½ cups (360ml) unsweetened Raspberry Juice
- 1 scoop (28g) Sugar-free Protein Powder
- 1 teaspoon (15ml) Vanilla Extract
- Pinch of Ground Cinnamon

Directions
Pour the raspberry juice and protein powder in your blender bottle and shake well until the protein powder is completely dissolved.

Add the remaining ingredients to the protein powder mixture and shake thoroughly until all ingredients are evenly

blended together.

Note: calories may vary slightly due to brands and other recipe modifications.

Deluxe Blackberry Shake

Use your freshly made blackberry juice with Greek yogurt and pecan butter to make a healthy and tasty drink. The great color and flavor of the blackberries will make this an irresistible shake.

Makes: 1 Serving
Preparation Time: 5 Minutes
479 Calories per serving

Ingredients

- 1 cup (240ml) unsweetened Blackberry Juice
- 1 scoop (28g) Sugar-free Protein Powder
- ½ cup (120ml) Fat-free Greek Yogurt
- 2 tablespoons (30g) Pecan Butter

Directions

Pour the blackberry juice and protein powder in your blender bottle and shake well until the protein powder is completely dissolved.

Add the remaining ingredients to the protein powder mixture and shake thoroughly until all ingredients are evenly blended together.

Note: calories may vary slightly due to brands and other recipe modifications.

Cranny Almond Shake

Unsweetened almond milk, a fantastic alternative to cow's milk, contains 2 grams of carbohydrates per cup, making it a great ingredient. The hint of cinnamon and nutmeg in this shake adds a lovely taste which you will have you looking forward to each sip.

Makes: *1 Serving*
Preparation Time: *5 Minutes*
192 Calories per serving

Ingredients

- 1 cup (240ml) unsweetened Almond Milk
- ½ cup (120ml) unsweetened Cranberry Juice
- 1 scoop (28g) Sugar-free Protein Powder
- ½ teaspoon (2.5g) Cinnamon Powder
- ¼ teaspoon (1g) Ground Nutmeg

Directions

Pour the milk, cranberry juice and protein powder in your blender bottle and shake well until the protein powder is completely dissolved.

Add the remaining ingredients to the protein powder mixture and shake thoroughly until all ingredients are evenly blended together.

Note: calories may vary slightly due to brands and other recipe modifications.

Pecan Prix Shake

Unsweetened soy milk is a great base for this shake, especially if you are on a lactose free diet. The addition of avocado helps to keep the carbohydrate levels in this shake low, as well as adds a lovely creamy texture.

Makes: 1 Serving
Preparation Time: 5 Minutes
550 Calories per serving

Ingredients

- 1 cup (240ml) organic unsweetened Soy Milk
- 1 scoop (28g) Sugar-free Protein Powder
- 1 large slice (100g) of Ripe Avocado, mashed until creamy
- 1 tablespoon (30g) Nut Butter

Directions

Pour the milk and protein powder in your blender bottle and shake well until the protein powder is completely dissolved.

Add the remaining ingredients to the protein powder mixture and shake thoroughly until all ingredients are evenly blended together.

Note: calories may vary slightly due to brands and other recipe

modifications.

Apple Fusion Shake

Apples are the theme of this shake! Unsweetened apple juice and sauce provides a great taste to this drink. The addition of cinnamon adds a nice hint of spice which will ensure this drink becomes one of your favorites.

Makes: *1 Serving*
Preparation Time: *5 Minutes*
261 Calories per serving

Ingredients
- 1 cup (240ml) unsweetened Apple Juice
- ¼ cup (60ml) filtered Water
- 1 scoop (28g) Sugar-free Protein Powder
- 2 tablespoons (30ml) unsweetened Applesauce
- 1 teaspoon (5g) Ground Cinnamon

Directions
Pour the apple juice and protein powder in your blender bottle and shake well until the protein powder is completely dissolved.

Add the remaining ingredients to the protein powder mixture and shake thoroughly until all ingredients are evenly blended together.

Note: calories may vary slightly due to brands and other recipe

modifications.

Creamy Blueberry Shake

If you can resist the urge to eat the blueberries whole, adding them to this shake makes a wonderfully healthy drink, as well as a wonderfully tasty one. The addition of avocado, almond milk and almond meal ensures this drink is low in carbohydrates and has a lovely creamy texture.

Makes: 1 *Serving*
Preparation Time: 5 *Minutes*
542 Calories per serving

Ingredients
- ½ cup (120ml) unsweetened Blueberry Juice
- ½ cup (120ml) unsweetened Almond Milk
- 1 scoop (28g) Sugar-free Protein Powder
- 1 large slice (100g) of Ripe Avocado, mashed until creamy
- ¼ cup (38g) Almond Meal

Directions
Pour the blueberry juice, almond milk and protein powder in your blender bottle and shake well until the protein powder is completely dissolved.

Add the remaining ingredients to the protein powder mixture and shake thoroughly until all ingredients are evenly blended together.

Note: calories may vary slightly due to brands and other recipe modifications.

Avocado Spinach Shake

This easily prepared shake has a nice creamy texture and great taste. The addition of chia seeds, a natural ingredient which aids your body in processing sugar, ensures this shake is very healthy and beneficial.

Makes: 1 Serving
Preparation Time: 5 Minutes
412 Calories per serving

Ingredients

- 1 cup (240ml) Skim Milk
- 1 scoop (28g) Sugar-free Protein Powder
- 1 large slice (100g) of Ripe Avocado, mashed until creamy
- 1 tablespoon (15g) Organic Spinach Powder
- 2 tablespoons (30g) Ground Chia Seeds

Directions

Pour the milk and protein powder in your blender bottle and shake well until the protein powder is completely dissolved.

Add the remaining ingredients to the protein powder mixture and shake thoroughly until all ingredients are evenly

blended together.

Note: calories may vary slightly due to brands and other recipe modifications.

Crème Berry Shake

Chia seeds which are believed to aid sugar regulation in the body, is combined with strawberry juice, yogurt and pecan butter in this shake. You will find this shake both delicious and beneficial, and this shake may also quickly become a firm favorite.

Makes: 1 Serving
Preparation Time: 5 Minutes
513 Calories per serving

Ingredients

- 1 cup (240ml) unsweetened Strawberry Juice
- 1 scoop (28g) Sugar-free Protein Powder
- ½ cup (120ml) Fat-free Yogurt
- 1 tablespoon (15g) Ground Chia Seeds
- 2 tablespoons (30g) Pecan Butter

Directions

Pour the juice and protein powder in your blender bottle and shake well until the protein powder is completely dissolved. Add the remaining ingredients to the protein powder

mixture and shake thoroughly until all ingredients are evenly blended together.

Note: calories may vary slightly due to brands and other recipe modifications.

PROTEIN SHAKES FOR KIDS

Vanilla Pumpkin Shake

If you have any problems getting your kids to try something different, then this shake will help you in your quest. The energy and nutrients provided by the maple syrup and almond milk make this a truly great drink.

Makes: *1 Serving*
Preparation Time: *5 Minutes*
226 Calories per serving

Ingredients
- ½ cup (120ml) Almond Milk
- ½ scoop (14g) Vanilla Protein Powder
- 1 cup (240ml) Pumpkin Puree
- 2 teaspoons (12ml) Pure Maple Syrup
- 1 teaspoon (6ml) Vanilla Extract

Directions
Pour the milk and protein powder in your blender bottle and shake well until the protein powder is completely dissolved.
Add the remaining ingredients to the protein powder

mixture and shake thoroughly until all ingredients are evenly blended together.

Note: calories may vary slightly due to brands and other recipe modifications.

Peanut Butter Jelly Shake

The classic sandwich of peanut butter and jelly is transformed into a wonderful shake with this recipe. Kids of all ages may be asking for this drink time and again.

Makes: 1 Serving
Preparation Time: 5 Minutes
480 Calories per serving

Ingredients
- ½ cup (120ml) Almond Milk
- ½ scoop (14g) Vanilla Protein Powder
- ½ cup (120ml) Strawberry Nectar
- ½ cup (120ml) Strawberry Yogurt
- 2 tablespoons (30g) Peanut Butter

Directions
Pour the milk and protein powder in your blender bottle and shake well until the protein powder is completely dissolved.

Add the remaining ingredients to the protein powder mixture and shake thoroughly until all ingredients are evenly blended together.

Note: calories may vary slightly due to brands and other recipe modifications.

Chocolate Pudding Shake

The delicious and sweet taste of chocolate, with added chia seeds makes this shake a great way to provide extra nutrients and proteins to your kids.

Makes: 1 Serving
Preparation Time: 5 Minutes
170 Calories per serving

Ingredients

- 1 cup (240ml) Whole Milk
- ½ scoop (14g) Chocolate Protein Powder
- 1 tablespoon (15g) Ground Chia Seeds
- 2 tablespoons (30g) Cocoa
- Honey or preferred sweetener to taste

Directions

Pour the milk and protein powder in your blender bottle and shake well until the protein powder is completely dissolved.

Add the remaining ingredients to the protein powder mixture and shake thoroughly until all ingredients are evenly blended together.

Note: calories may vary slightly due to brands and other recipe modifications.

Fruity Pie Shake

The exotic flavors of pineapple and mango, combined with the health benefits of banana and chia seeds makes this shake truly healthy. The energy boost that this shake gives to your kids makes it a perfect drink in preparation for physical activities.

Makes: 1 Serving
Preparation Time: 5 Minutes
270.5 Calories per serving

Ingredients

- ½ cup (120ml) Pineapple Juice
- ¼ cup (60ml) Mango Juice
- ½ scoop (14g) Vanilla Protein Powder
- ½ of a large Banana, mashed
- ½ cup (120ml) Banana Cream Pie Yogurt
- 1 tablespoon (15g) Chia Seeds

Directions

Pour the pineapple juice, mango juice and protein powder in your blender bottle and shake well until the protein powder is completely dissolved.

Add the remaining ingredients to the protein powder mixture and shake thoroughly until all ingredients are evenly blended together.

Note: calories may vary slightly due to brands and other recipe modifications.

Healthy Green Shake

Many kids refuse to eat their greens at the table. This shake will help all parents to add the goodness of greens to their kid's diet by incorporating spinach in this recipe. The added iron into your kid's diet will benefit them greatly.

Makes: *1 Serving*
Preparation Time: *5 Minutes*
201 Calories per serving

Ingredients
- 1 cup (240ml) Almond Milk (or use your preferred milk)
- ½ scoop (14g) Vanilla Protein Powder
- 1 tablespoon (15g) Organic Spinach Powder
- ½ of a large Banana, mashed
- Preferred Sweetener to taste

Directions
Pour the milk and protein powder in your blender bottle and shake well until the protein powder is completely dissolved.

Add the remaining ingredients to the protein powder mixture and shake thoroughly until all ingredients are evenly blended together.

Note: calories may vary slightly due to brands and other recipe modifications.

Berry Brainy Shake

This recipe combines pomegranate juice and mashed avocado, two of the healthiest fruits available. The vitamin boost your kids will get from this shake is truly amazing. Your kids will find the flavors of this shake equally amazing.

Makes: *1 Serving*
Preparation Time: *5 Minutes*
431 Calories per serving

Ingredients

- ½ cup (120ml) Blueberry Juice
- ½ cup (120ml) Pomegranate Juice
- ½ cup (120ml) Almond Milk
- ½ scoop (14g) Vanilla Protein Powder
- 1 large slice (100g) of Ripe Avocado, mashed until creamy

Directions

Pour the juices, milk and protein powder in your blender bottle and shake well until the protein powder is completely dissolved.

Add the remaining ingredients to the protein powder mixture and shake thoroughly until all ingredients are evenly blended together.

Note: calories may vary slightly due to brands and other recipe modifications.

Pineapple Spinach Shake

Kids of all ages will enjoy this recipe which incorporates piña colada yogurt. The creamy texture of this shake, coupled with the strong pineapple taste will make this a favorite for any time of the day.

Makes: *1 Serving*
Preparation Time: *5 Minutes*
218 Calories per serving

Ingredients

- ¼ cup (60ml) Pineapple Juice
- ½ scoop (14g) Vanilla Protein Powder
- ½ cup (120ml) Piña Colada Yogurt
- 1 tablespoon (15g) Organic Spinach Powder

Directions

Pour the pineapple juice and protein powder in your blender bottle and shake well until the protein powder is completely dissolved.

Add the remaining ingredients to the protein powder mixture and shake thoroughly until all ingredients are evenly blended together.

Note: calories may vary slightly due to brands and other recipe modifications.

Tropical Kiddies Pie Shake

Your kids will enjoy making this shake time and again, and will benefit from the added vitamins and proteins gained from the tropical ingredients.

Makes: *1 Serving*
Preparation Time: *5 Minutes*
302 Calories per serving

Ingredients

- ¼ cup (60ml) Organic Unsweetened Coconut Milk
- ½ cup (120ml) Mango Juice
- ½ scoop (14g) Vanilla Protein Powder
- ½ cup (120ml) Banana Cream Pie Yogurt

Directions

Pour the coconut milk, mango juice and protein powder in your blender bottle and shake well until the protein powder is completely dissolved.

Add the remaining ingredient to the protein powder mixture and shake thoroughly until all ingredients are evenly blended together.

<u>Note:</u> calories may vary slightly due to brands and other recipe modifications.

Orange Strawberry Shake

This delicious strawberry colored shake will be a big hit at snack times. The energy and vitamin boost that this shake will provide will help your kids stay active all day long.

Makes: 1 Serving
Preparation Time: 5 Minutes
258 Calories per serving

Ingredients

- ½ cup (120ml) Orange Juice
- ½ scoop (14g) Vanilla Protein Powder
- ½ cup (120ml) Strawberry Nectar
- ¼ cup (60ml) Strawberry Yogurt

Directions

Pour the orange juice and protein powder in your blender bottle and shake well until the protein powder is completely dissolved.

Add the remaining ingredients to the protein powder mixture and shake thoroughly until all ingredients are evenly blended together.

Note: calories may vary slightly due to brands and other recipe modifications.

Anti-Flu Skittles Shake

The variety of colors that make up this shake gives it its fun name. The boost of vitamins and proteins provided by the fruit juices and the chia seeds makes this a great drink when flu season arrives.

Makes: 1 Serving
Preparation Time: 5 Minutes
246.5 Calories per serving

Ingredients

- ½ cup (120ml) unsweetened Pomegranate Juice
- ½ cup (120ml) unsweetened Blackberry Juice
- ½ cup (120ml) unsweetened Orange Juice
- ½ scoop (14g) Vanilla Protein Powder
- 1 tablespoon (15g) Ground Chia Seeds

Directions

Pour the juices and protein powder in your blender bottle and shake well until the protein powder is completely dissolved.

Add the remaining ingredient to the protein powder mixture and shake thoroughly until all ingredients are evenly blended together.

Note: calories may vary slightly due to brands and other recipe modifications.

Berry Jiggles Shake

The combination of berries with protein powder ensures your child will receive a healthy dose of vitamins. The addition of flax seeds also ensures an extra helping of omega 3 fatty acids and fiber into your kid's diet.

Makes: 1 Serving
Preparation Time: 5 Minutes
280.5 Calories per serving

Ingredients

- ½ cup (120ml) unsweetened Blueberry Juice
- ½ cup (120ml) unsweetened Blackberry Juice
- ½ cup (120ml) unsweetened Raspberry Juice
- ½ scoop (14g) Vanilla Protein Powder
- 1 tablespoon (15g) Ground Flax Seed

Directions

Pour the juices and protein powder in your blender bottle and shake well until the protein powder is completely dissolved.

Add the remaining ingredients to the protein powder mixture and shake thoroughly until all ingredients are evenly blended together.

Note: calories may vary slightly due to brands and other recipe modifications.

Pomegranate Surprise Shake

It is fun to make this shake and ask your kids to guess the contents. As well as being a great shake to test their taste buds, this shake will also provide an abundance of essential nutrients and protein into their diet.

Makes: *1 Serving*
Preparation Time: *5 Minutes*
362 Calories per serving

Ingredients

- ½ cup (120ml) unsweetened Pomegranate Juice
- ½ scoop (14g) Protein Powder
- ½ cup (120ml) Piña Colada Yogurt
- 1 tablespoon (15ml) Flax Seed Oil
- Sweeten to taste (optional)

Directions

Pour the pomegranate juice and protein powder in your blender bottle and shake well until the protein powder is completely dissolved.

Add the remaining ingredients to the protein powder mixture and shake thoroughly until all ingredients are evenly blended together.

Note: calories may vary slightly due to brands and other recipe modifications.

Maple Almond Crush Shake

A double of dose of almond in this shake ensure your kids receive healthy fats into their diet. The addition of maple syrup ensures this shake has a sweet taste, making it a great treat for after school.

Makes: *1 Serving*
Preparation Time: *5 Minutes*
302 Calories per serving

Ingredients

- ½ cup (120ml) Almond Milk
- ½ scoop (14g) Vanilla Protein Powder
- 1 teaspoon (6ml) Maple Syrup
- 1 tablespoon (15g) Almond Butter
- ½ cup (120ml) Vanilla Yogurt

Directions

Pour the milk and protein powder in your blender bottle and shake well until the protein powder is completely dissolved.

Add the remaining ingredients to the protein powder mixture and shake thoroughly until all ingredients are evenly blended together.

Note: calories may vary slightly due to brands and other recipe modifications.

BRAIN HEALTHY SHAKES

Blueberry Apple Shake

Ensure you take care of your brain's health by drinking this shake regularly. The ingredients provide a great source of vitamins, all of which will aid in keeping a healthy brain.

Makes: *1 Serving*
Preparation Time: *5 Minutes*
420 Calories per serving

Ingredients

- 1 cup (240ml) unsweetened Apple Juice
- ½ cup (120ml) unsweetened Blueberry Juice
- 1 scoop (28g) Protein Powder
- 2 tablespoons (30g) Hemp Powder
- 1 teaspoon (5ml) Organic Virgin Coconut Oil

Directions

Pour the juices and protein powder in your blender bottle

and shake well until the protein powder is completely dissolved.

Add the remaining ingredients to the protein powder mixture and shake thoroughly until all ingredients are evenly blended together.

Note: calories may vary slightly due to brands and other recipe modifications.

Strawberry Coconut Shake

With coconut having a wide variety of health benefits, especially in keeping your brain healthy, this shake is a great way to ensure you are helping to look after your brain through the years. The addition of strawberry juice and chia seeds also adds extra vitamins to this drink.

Makes: 1 Serving
Preparation Time: 5 Minutes
460 Calories per serving

Ingredients
- ½ cup (120ml) Organic Unsweetened Coconut Milk
- ½ cup (120ml) unsweetened Strawberry Juice
- 1 scoop (28g) Protein Powder
- 2 tablespoons (30g) Ground Chia Seeds

Directions
Pour the coconut milk, strawberry juice and protein powder

in your blender bottle and shake well until the protein powder is completely dissolved.

Add the remaining ingredient to the protein powder mixture and shake thoroughly until all ingredients are evenly blended together.

Note: calories may vary slightly due to brands and other recipe modifications.

Mixed Berry Shake

Blueberries are believed to be effective in delaying or reducing short-term memory loss. The benefits of this berry are provided in this shake, along with the vitamins and proteins provided by the other ingredients.

Makes: *1 Serving*
Preparation Time: *5 Minutes*
485 Calories per serving

Ingredients

- ¾ cup (180) unsweetened Blueberry Juice
- ½ cup (120ml) unsweetened Raspberry Juice
- 1 scoop (28g) Protein Powder
- 2 tablespoons (30g) raw organic Almond Butter
- 1 tablespoon (15g) Ground Chia Seeds

Directions

Pour the juices and protein powder in your blender bottle and shake well until the protein powder is completely dissolved.

Add the remaining ingredients to the protein powder mixture and shake thoroughly until all ingredients are evenly blended together.

Note: calories may vary slightly due to brands and other recipe modifications.

Acai Power Shake

Acai is believed to be a neuro-protector, so indulge in this shake often to benefit from the goodness of these seeds. The combination with the other ingredients also ensures you receive a healthy dose of vitamins, all working to keep your brain healthy.

Makes: 1 Serving
Preparation Time: 5 Minutes
508.5 Calories per serving

Ingredients
- ¾ cup (180ml) unsweetened Almond Milk
- ½ cup (120ml) unsweetened Acai Berry Juice
- 1 scoop (28g) Protein Powder
- 1 tablespoon (15g) Flaxseed Meal
- ½ teaspoon (5g) Ground Cinnamon
- 1 large slice (100g) of Ripe Avocado, mashed until creamy

Directions
Pour the milk, acai juice and protein powder in your blender

bottle and shake well until the protein powder is completely dissolved.

Add the remaining ingredients to the protein powder mixture and shake thoroughly until all ingredients are evenly blended together.

Note: calories may vary slightly due to brands and other recipe modifications.

Pomegranate Strawberry Shake

Pomegranate juice is believed to increase blood flow to the brain and help in improving your memory. This shake, therefore, is a great brain food which is rich in vitamins and protein. The delicious strawberry flavor will leave you wanting more of this drink.

Makes: *1 Serving*
Preparation Time: *5 Minutes*
410 Calories per serving

Ingredients

- ¼ cup (60ml) unsweetened Pomegranate Juice
- ¾ cup (180ml) unsweetened Strawberry Juice
- 1 scoop (28g) Protein Powder
- ¼ cup (60ml) Fat Free Strawberry Yogurt
- 1 tablespoon (15g) Flaxseed Oil
- Natural Stevia to taste

Directions

Pour the juices and protein powder in your blender bottle and shake well until the protein powder is completely dissolved.

Add the remaining ingredients to the protein powder mixture and shake thoroughly until all ingredients are evenly blended together.

Note: calories may vary slightly due to brands and other recipe modifications.

Mango Avocado Shake

Spinach, a good source of folic acid which helps against brain shrinkage with age, is a key ingredient in this healthy shake. With the combination of mango juice, a good source of vitamin B6 and almond milk, this shake is a great way for you to look after your brain.

Makes: *1 Serving*
Preparation Time: *5 Minutes*
439 Calories per serving

Ingredients

- ½ cup (120ml) unsweetened Mango Juice
- 1 cup (180ml) unsweetened Almond Milk
- 1 scoop (28g) Vanilla Protein Powder
- 2 tablespoons (30g) Organic Spinach Powder

- 1 large slice (100g) of Ripe Avocado, mashed until creamy

Directions

Pour the mango juice, almond milk and protein powder in your blender bottle and shake well until the protein powder is completely dissolved.

Add the remaining ingredients to the protein powder mixture and shake thoroughly until all ingredients are evenly blended together.

Note: calories may vary slightly due to brands and other recipe modifications.

Blueberry Beet Shake

This easy to make shake has a good variety of foods which makes this a great tasting drink. Each ingredient in this recipe contains vitamins proven to aid a healthy brain.

Makes: 1 Serving
Preparation Time: 5 Minutes
340 Calories per serving

Ingredients

- ¾ cup (180ml) unsweetened Almond Milk
- ½ cup (120ml) unsweetened Blueberry Juice
- 1 scoop (28g) Vanilla Protein Powder
- ¼ cup (60ml) unsweetened

Applesauce
- 2 tablespoons (30g) Organic Beet Powder
- Dash of Ground Ginger

Directions

Pour the milk, blueberry juice and protein powder in your blender bottle and shake well until the protein powder is completely dissolved.

Add the remaining ingredients to the protein powder mixture and shake thoroughly until all ingredients are evenly blended together.

Note: calories may vary slightly due to brands and other recipe modifications.

Blueberry Almond Shake

Blueberries are a great health food for your brain and are combined with almond in this shake to make a drink high in vitamins. It is especially high in vitamin E which is linked to reducing cognitive decline with age. You will love this shake and the benefits to your brain health.

Makes: 1 Serving
Preparation Time: 5 Minutes
357 Calories per serving

Ingredients

- ¾ cup (180ml) unsweetened Blueberry Juice

- ½ cup (120ml) unsweetened Almond Milk
- 1 tablespoon (15g) raw organic Almond Butter
- 1 scoop (28g) Protein Powder
- Natural Stevia to taste

Directions

Pour the blueberry juice, almond milk and protein powder in your blender bottle and shake well until the protein powder is completely dissolved.

Add the remaining ingredients to the protein powder mixture and shake thoroughly until all ingredients are evenly blended together.

Note: calories may vary slightly due to brands and other recipe modifications.

Grapefruit Coco Shake

The use of grapefruit juice in this shake adds a lovely citrus flavor. Grapefruits have also been linked to mental sharpness, thus this ingredient, combined with coconut water and applesauce ensures that you are giving your brain the best foods to ensure its continued health.

Makes: *1 Serving*
Preparation Time: *5 Minutes*
279 Calories per serving

Ingredients

- ½ cup (120ml) unsweetened Organic Coconut Water
- ½ cup (120ml) unsweetened Grapefruit Juice
- 1 scoop (28g) Protein Powder
- ½ cup (120ml) unsweetened Applesauce
- Natural Stevia to taste

Directions

Pour the coconut water, grapefruit juice and protein powder in your blender bottle and shake well until the protein powder is completely dissolved.

Add the remaining ingredients to the protein powder mixture and shake thoroughly until all ingredients are evenly blended together.

Note: calories may vary slightly due to brands and other recipe modifications.

Cherry Almond Shake

Having this shake is a great way to ensure you receive your daily dose of vitamin E. The addition of cherry juice adds a fruity sweetness and is also a natural ingredient which aids sleep. Have this shake before bedtime, have a good rest and be ready for the world the next day.

Makes: *1 Serving*
Preparation Time: *5 Minutes*

363 Calories per serving

Ingredients

- ½ cup (120ml) unsweetened Almond Milk
- ¾ cup (180ml) unsweetened Cherry Juice
- 1 scoop (28g) Vanilla Protein Powder
- 1 tablespoon (15g) raw organic Almond Butter
- Dash of Ground Cinnamon

Directions

Pour the almond milk, cherry juice and protein powder in your blender bottle and shake well until the protein powder is completely dissolved.

Add the remaining ingredients to the protein powder mixture and shake thoroughly until all ingredients are evenly blended together.

Note: calories may vary slightly due to brands and other recipe modifications.

Winter Green Shake

Help to reduce your blood pressure, and therefore increase blood flow to your brain by ensuring you have a daily dose of avocado with this delicious shake. The added benefits of apple juice and spinach will also ensure your brain gets the extra vitamins and folic acid to keep it healthy.

Makes: 1 Serving
Preparation Time: 5 Minutes
514 Calories per serving

Ingredients

- ¾ cup (180ml) unsweetened Apple Juice
- 1 scoop (28g) Vanilla Protein Powder
- ½ cup (120ml) Vanilla Yogurt
- 2 tablespoons (30g) Organic Spinach Powder
- 1 large slice (100g) of Ripe Avocado, mashed until creamy

Directions

Pour the apple juice and protein powder in your blender bottle and shake well until the protein powder is completely dissolved.

Add the remaining ingredients to the protein powder mixture and shake thoroughly until all ingredients are evenly blended together.

Note: calories may vary slightly due to brands and other recipe modifications.

Cranberry Twister Shake

This delicious and easily prepared shake will ensure you are giving your brain the best in life. The extra boost of vitamins provided by these specially chosen ingredients will help you rest better knowing that you are looking after your brain as well as your overall health while having this drink.

Makes: 1 *Serving*
Preparation Time: 5 *Minutes*
358 Calories per serving

Ingredients

- ¾ cup (180ml) unsweetened Strawberry Juice
- ½ cup (120ml) unsweetened Cranberry Juice
- 1 Scoop (28g) Vanilla Protein Powder
- 3 teaspoon (15ml) Flaxseed Oil

Directions

Pour the juices and protein powder in your blender bottle and shake well until the protein powder is completely dissolved.

Add the remaining ingredient to the protein powder mixture and shake thoroughly until all ingredients are evenly blended together.

Note: calories may vary slightly due to brands and other recipe modifications.

Simply Orange Banana Shake

The sweetness of orange adds to the wonderful taste in this drink, as well as provides a great source of vitamin C. This shake will not only help to keep your brain healthy, it will also revitalize you after a hard day's work.

Makes: *1 Serving*
Preparation Time: *5 Minutes*
379 Calories per serving

Ingredients

- 1 cup (240ml) unsweetened Orange Juice
- 1 scoop (28g) Vanilla Protein Powder
- ½ of a large Banana, mashed
- 2 teaspoons (10ml) Organic Virgin Coconut Oil

Directions

Pour the orange juice and protein powder in your blender bottle and shake well until the protein powder is completely dissolved.

Add the remaining ingredients to the protein powder mixture and shake thoroughly until all ingredients are evenly blended together.

<u>Note:</u> calories may vary slightly due to brands and other recipe modifications.

Carrot Coconut Shake

Did you know that carrots are a great brain food, and are not just good for your eyes? Adding carrot juice into your diet will introduce an antioxidant which aids in reducing inflammation which is believed to be linked to brain deterioration. Coconut milk and banana adds a nice flavor to this drink, as well as providing vitamins and nutrients.

Makes: *1 Serving*
Preparation Time: *5 Minutes*
503 Calories per serving

Ingredients

- ½ cup (120ml) unsweetened Organic Coconut Milk
- ½ cup (120ml) unsweetened Carrot Juice
- 1 scoop (28g) Vanilla Protein Powder
- ½ of a large Banana, mashed

Directions

Pour the coconut milk, carrot juice and protein powder in your blender bottle and shake well until the protein powder is completely dissolved.

Add the remaining ingredient to the protein powder mixture and shake thoroughly until all ingredients are evenly blended together.

Note: calories may vary slightly due to brands and other recipe modifications.

Go-Easy Blackberry Shake

As the name suggests, this easily prepared shake has a great blackberry flavor. Blackberries are believed to aid in combating age related memory loss. Coupled with the benefits of avocado, this shake not only aids a healthy brain, it also tastes great and creamy.

Makes: 1 Serving
Preparation Time: 5 Minutes
387.5 Calories per serving

Ingredients
- ½ cup (120ml) unsweetened Blackberry Juice
- ½ cup (120ml) unsweetened Almond Milk
- 1 scoop (28g) Protein Powder
- 1 large slice (100g) of Ripe Avocado, mashed until creamy

Directions
Pour the blackberry juice, almond milk and protein powder in your blender bottle and shake well until the protein powder is completely dissolved.

Add the remaining ingredient to the protein powder mixture and shake thoroughly until all ingredients are evenly blended together.

Note: calories may vary slightly due to brands and other recipe modifications.

PROTEIN SHAKES FOR WEIGHT GAIN

Orange Cream Shake

If you love cream, this shake will quickly be top of your list. The heavy cream combined with orange juice and whole milk makes this shake truly tasty, and very indulgent.

Makes: 1 *Serving*
Preparation Time: 5 *Minutes*
353 Calories per serving

Ingredients
- ½ cup (120ml) Whole Milk
- ½ cup (120ml) Orange Juice
- 1 scoop (28g) Protein Powder
- ¼ cup (60ml) Heavy Cream

Directions

Pour the milk, orange juice and protein powder in your blender bottle and shake well until the protein powder is completely dissolved.

Add the remaining ingredients to the protein powder

mixture and shake thoroughly until all ingredients are evenly blended together.

Note: calories may vary slightly due to brands and other recipe modifications.

Double Chocolate Almond Shake

Help add a few extra pounds by having this shake on a regular basis. The combination of double chocolate, almond butter and whole milk makes this a deliciously creamy drink, ideal for times when you need a quick chocolate hit to perk you up.

Makes: *1 Serving*
Preparation Time: *10 Minutes*
595 Calories per serving

Ingredients
- 1 cup (240ml) Whole Milk
- 1 scoop (28g) Chocolate Protein Powder
- ½ cup (120ml) Chocolate Yogurt
- 2 tablespoon (30g) Almond Butter

Directions
Pour the milk and protein powder in your blender bottle and shake well until the protein powder is completely dissolved.

Add the remaining ingredients to the protein powder mixture and shake thoroughly until all ingredients are evenly blended together.

Note: calories may vary slightly due to brands and other recipe

modifications.

Minty Ice Cream Shake

Substitute this shake for a dessert after dinner and you'll be in for a treat! The ice cream, milk and mint extract makes this a creamy, smooth and refreshing drink. This drink will be a hit in the summer months when the temperatures are rising.

Makes: 1 Serving
Preparation Time: 5 Minutes
412 Calories per serving

Ingredients

- 1 cup (240ml) Whole Milk
- 1 scoop (28g) Protein Powder
- ½ cup (120ml) Vanilla Ice Cream
- ¼ teaspoon (1.5ml) Mint Extract

Directions

Pour the milk and protein powder in your blender bottle and shake well until the protein powder is completely dissolved.

Add the remaining ingredients to the protein powder mixture and shake thoroughly until all ingredients are evenly blended together.

Note: calories may vary slightly due to brands and other recipe modifications.

Banana Strawberry Pudding Shake

The fantastic flavors of strawberry and banana are combined in this shake. Not only will this shake help you in putting on a few pounds, it will also give you an energy boost to help you through the day.

Makes: 1 Serving
Preparation Time: 5 Minutes
432.5 Calories per serving

Ingredients

- ¾ cup (180ml) Whole Milk
- 1 scoop (28g) Protein Powder
- ¼ cup (60ml) Strawberry Nectar
- ¼ cup (60ml) Heavy Cream
- ½ of a large Banana, mashed

Directions

Pour the milk and protein powder in your blender bottle and shake well until the protein powder is completely dissolved.

Add the remaining ingredients to the protein powder mixture and shake thoroughly until all ingredients are evenly blended together.

Note: calories may vary slightly due to brands and other recipe modifications.

Creamy Pineapple Shake

Pineapple juice and coconut milk gives this shake a tropical flavor. As well as helping you put on weight, this shake is packed with vitamins and proteins to help keep you healthy.

Makes: *1 Serving*
Preparation Time: *5 Minutes*
398 Calories per serving

Ingredients

- ½ cup (120ml) Whole Milk
- ¼ cup (60ml) Coconut Milk
- ½ cup (120ml) Pineapple Juice
- 1 Scoop (28g) Protein Powder
- ¼ teaspoon (1.25g) Ground Cinnamon

Directions

Pour the whole milk, coconut milk and pineapple juice and protein powder in your blender bottle and shake well until the protein powder is completely dissolved.

Add the remaining ingredient to the protein powder mixture and shake thoroughly until all ingredients are evenly blended together.

Note: calories may vary slightly due to brands and other recipe modifications.

Coffee-Caramel Shake

Ditch the regular coffee and have this fantastic coffee-caramel shake! Substitute your coffee for this shake and enjoy the great taste, the health benefits of almond milk, as well as adding that bit of extra weight you desire. You will find this shake so delicious that you'll wonder why you bothered with normal coffee!

Makes: 1 Serving
Preparation Time: 5 Minutes
277 Calories per serving

Ingredients

- ¾ cup (180ml) Almond Milk (or use milk of your choice)
- 1 Scoop (28g) Chocolate Protein Powder
- 2 tablespoons (30ml) Caramel Topping
- ½ Cup (120ml) Brewed Coffee, cooled and chilled
- ½ cup (120ml) Cream Pie Yogurt

Directions

Pour the milk and protein powder in your blender bottle and shake well until the protein powder is completely dissolved.

Add the remaining ingredients to the protein powder mixture and shake thoroughly until all ingredients are evenly blended together.

Note: calories may vary slightly due to brands and other recipe modifications.

Banana Oatmeal Shake

This high calorie shake will make you feel like you've eaten dinner and dessert in a glass! The ground oatmeal adds a lovely texture to this drink, and the banana ensures you get a good dose of energy.

Makes: *1 Serving*
Preparation Time: *5 Minutes*
591 Calories per serving

Ingredients

- ½ cup (120ml) Whole Milk
- 1 scoop (28g) Vanilla Protein Powder
- ¼ cup (60ml) Heavy Cream
- 4 tablespoons (60g) Ground Oatmeal
- ½ of a large Banana, mashed
- Sweeten to taste

Directions

Pour the milk and protein powder in your blender bottle and shake well until the protein powder is completely dissolved.

Add the remaining ingredients to the protein powder mixture and shake thoroughly until all ingredients are evenly blended together.

Note: calories may vary slightly due to brands and other recipe modifications.

Peanut Butter Banana Shake

This is another high calorie shake which will help you stay healthy in your weight gaining program. The ground flaxseed, peanut butter and banana add fiber, nutrients and vitamins to your daily diet.

Makes: 1 Serving
Preparation Time: 5 Minutes
669 Calories per serving

Ingredients

- 1 cup (240ml) Whole Milk
- 1 scoop (28g) Vanilla Protein Powder
- ½ of a large Banana, mashed
- ¼ cup (38g) Ground Flaxseed
- 2 tablespoons (30g) Peanut Butter

Directions

Pour the milk and protein powder in your blender bottle and shake well until the protein powder is completely dissolved.

Add the remaining ingredients to the protein powder mixture and shake thoroughly until all ingredients are evenly blended together.

Note: calories may vary slightly due to brands and other recipe modifications.

Rich Protein Chocolate Shake

The addition of egg whites in this shake ensures that the protein levels are high. This amazing shake will help you with your weight gain as well as making you feel like you are having a treat!

Makes: *1 Serving*
Preparation Time: *5 Minutes*
593 Calories per serving

Ingredients

- ½ cup (120ml) Organic Coconut Milk
- ½ cup (120ml) Whole Milk
- 1 Scoop (28g) Chocolate Protein Powder
- ½ cup (120ml) Chocolate Yogurt
- 4 Egg Whites

Directions

Pour the coconut milk, whole milk and protein powder in your blender bottle and shake well until the protein powder is completely dissolved.

Add the remaining ingredients to the protein powder mixture and shake thoroughly until all ingredients are evenly blended together.

Note: calories may vary slightly due to brands and other recipe modifications.

Cinnamon Flax Milk Shake

This milk shake not only benefits from the taste of cinnamon, but it also boasts a great source of omega-3 fatty acids from the flaxseed oil. This shake will quickly become a favorite while you strive to gain more weight.

Makes: *1 Serving*
Preparation Time: *5 Minutes*
406 Calories per serving

Ingredients

- 1 cup (240ml) Whole Milk
- 1 scoop (28g) Vanilla Protein Powder
- 1 teaspoon (5g) Ground Cinnamon
- 3 teaspoons (15ml) Flaxseed Oil

Directions

Pour the milk and protein powder in your blender bottle and shake well until the protein powder is completely dissolved.

Add the remaining ingredients to the protein powder mixture and shake thoroughly until all ingredients are evenly blended together.

Note: calories may vary slightly due to brands and other recipe modifications.

Strawberry Jelly Shake

The combination of strawberry nectar, yogurt and pecan butter makes a creamy shake with a crunchy texture. You'll not only love the feel of this shake in your mouth, you'll also love the taste and you will want to have it time and again.

Makes: *1 Serving*
Preparation Time: *5 Minutes*
593 Calories per serving

Ingredients

- ½ cup (120ml) Whole Milk
- 1 scoop (28g) Protein Powder
- ½ cup (120ml) Strawberry Nectar
- ½ cup (120ml) Strawberry Yogurt
- 2 tablespoon (30ml) Pecan Butter (or use your favorite nut butter)

Directions

Pour the milk and protein powder in your blender bottle and shake well until the protein powder is completely dissolved.

Add the remaining ingredients to the protein powder mixture and shake thoroughly until all ingredients are evenly blended together.

Note: calories may vary slightly due to brands and other recipe modifications.

Creamy Avocado Chocolate Shake

Avocados are a great source of healthy fat and calories. Adding this ingredient into this shake makes this a truly healthy drink. The addition of heavy whipping cream will make this shake extra creamy, and this will also help with your weight gain goals.

Makes: *1 Serving*
Preparation Time: *5 Minutes*
445 Calories per serving

Ingredients

- 1 cup (240ml) Whole Milk
- 1 scoop (28g) Chocolate Protein Powder
- 1 tablespoon (15g) Heavy Whipping Cream
- 1 large slice (100g) of Ripe Avocado, mashed until creamy
- Sweeten to taste

Directions

Pour the milk and protein powder in your blender bottle and shake well until the protein powder is completely dissolved.

Add the remaining ingredients to the protein powder mixture and shake thoroughly until all ingredients are evenly blended together.

Note: calories may vary slightly due to brands and other recipe modifications.

Triple Berry Coffee Shake

This triple berry coffee shake combines the smooth taste of coffee with a fantastic yogurt. This shake is ideal for a mid-morning treat.

Makes: *1 Serving*
Preparation Time: *5 Minutes*
341.5 Calories per serving

Ingredients

- 1 cup (240ml) Whole Milk
- 1 scoop (28g) Protein Powder
- ½ cup (120ml) Triple Berry Yogurt
- ½ cup (120ml) Brewed Coffee, cooled and chilled

Directions

Pour the milk and protein powder in your blender bottle and shake well until the protein powder is completely dissolved.

Add the remaining ingredients to the protein powder mixture and shake thoroughly until all ingredients are evenly blended together.

Note: calories may vary slightly due to brands and other recipe modifications.

Smooth Sizzler Shake

This smooth shake has a delicious vanilla taste mixed with nut butter smoothness. You will find this shake irresistible once you have tried it and you may be sharing this recipe with your friends too. The nutritious content will also help you with your aim to gain a few pounds.

Makes: *1 Serving*
Preparation Time: *5 Minutes*
464 Calories per serving

Ingredients

- 1 cup (240ml) Whole Milk
- 1 scoop (28g) Vanilla Protein Powder
- ½ cup (120ml) Vanilla Yogurt
- 1 tablespoon (15g) raw organic Nut Butter (pecan, almond or coconut)
- ¼ teaspoon (1.5g) Mint Extract
- Sweeten to taste

Directions

Pour the milk and protein powder in your blender bottle and shake well until the protein powder is completely dissolved.

Add the remaining ingredients to the protein powder mixture and shake thoroughly until all ingredients are evenly blended together.

Note: calories may vary slightly due to brands and other recipe modifications.

Mango Cream Pie Shake

The fantastic combination of banana, yogurt and mango juice makes this smooth shake perfect for a mid-afternoon treat. Find a quiet spot to enjoy this shake while you re-energize for the evening ahead.

Makes: *1 Serving*
Preparation Time: *5 Minutes*
352 Calories per serving

Ingredients

- ½ cup (120ml) Whole Milk
- ½ cup (120ml) Mango Juice
- 1 scoop (28g) Protein Powder
- ½ cup (120ml) Banana Cream Pie Yogurt
- ½ of a large Banana, mashed

Directions

Pour the milk, mango juice and protein powder in your blender bottle and shake well until the protein powder is completely dissolved.

Add the remaining ingredients to the protein powder mixture and shake thoroughly until all ingredients are evenly blended together.

Note: calories may vary slightly due to brands and other recipe modifications.

PROTEIN SHAKES FOR DINNER

Banana Power Shake

Banana, oatmeal and flax seed are combined to make a great energy boosting power shake which is ideal for anytime of the day or when you are feeling a little low. The vitamins and proteins from these ingredients, coupled with the energy release, will be a great "pick-me-up".

Makes: 1 Serving
Preparation Time: 5 Minutes
533 Calories per serving

Ingredients
- 1 cup (240ml) Skim Milk
- 1 scoop (28g) Protein Powder
- ½ of a large Banana, mashed
- 4 tablespoons (60g) Ground Oatmeal
- 1 tablespoon (15g) Ground Flax Seed

Directions
Pour the milk and protein powder in your blender bottle and shake well until the protein powder is completely dissolved.

Add the remaining ingredients to the protein powder mixture and shake thoroughly until all ingredients are evenly blended together.

Note: calories may vary slightly due to brands and other recipe modifications.

Vanilla Pumpkin Shake

This shake has a great taste and texture from pureed pumpkin, as well as being full of antioxidants and a good source of vitamin A. This is a lovely drink to add to your dinner time shake menu.

Makes: 1 Serving
Preparation Time: 5 Minutes
302 Calories per serving

Ingredients

- 1 cup (240ml) Soy Milk (or use milk of your choice)
- 1 scoop (28g) Vanilla Protein Powder
- ½ cup (120ml) Pumpkin Puree
- Cinnamon to taste
- Nutmeg to taste
- Sweeten to taste

Directions

Pour the milk and protein powder in your blender bottle and shake well until the protein powder is completely dissolved.

Add the remaining ingredients to the protein powder mixture and shake thoroughly until all ingredients are evenly

blended together.

Note: calories may vary slightly due to brands and other recipe modifications.

Blueberry Banana Fix Shake

The health benefits of blueberries, coupled with the energy provided by banana, make this a healthy and energizing shake. This drink will provide the energy boost to tackle any problem after a relaxing dinner.

Makes: 1 Serving
Preparation Time: 5 Minutes
341 Calories per serving

Ingredients

- 1 cup (240ml) Skim Milk
- ½ cup (120ml) unsweetened Blueberry Juice
- 1 scoop (28g) Protein Powder
- ½ of a large Banana, mashed
- Sweeten to taste

Directions

Pour the milk, blueberry juice and protein powder in your blender bottle and shake well until the protein powder is completely dissolved.

Add the remaining ingredients to the protein powder mixture and shake thoroughly until all ingredients are evenly

blended together.

Note: calories may vary slightly due to brands and other recipe modifications.

Deluxe Vanilla Shake

Vanilla protein powder and vanilla extract give this shake an unmistakable vanilla taste. The addition of Piña colada yogurt adds an exotic taste which will leave you feeling relaxed after a hard day at work.

Makes: 1 Serving
Preparation Time: 5 Minutes
337 Calories per serving

Ingredients

- 1 cup (240ml) Skim Milk
- 1 scoop (28g) Vanilla Protein Powder
- 1 teaspoon (5ml) Vanilla Extract
- ½ cup (120ml) Piña Colada Yogurt
- 1 tablespoon (15g) Ground Chia Seeds

Directions

Pour the milk and protein powder in your blender bottle and shake well until the protein powder is completely dissolved.

Add the remaining ingredients to the protein powder mixture and shake thoroughly until all ingredients are evenly blended together.

Note: calories may vary slightly due to brands and other recipe modifications.

Strawberry Chocolate Shake

You may have asked what could be more delicious than chocolate covered strawberries. Well, this shake is just as tasty and has the added bonus of being packed with other essential nutrients. This is the ideal shake to end a wonderful dinner.

Makes: 1 Serving
Preparation Time: 5 Minutes
355 Calories per serving

Ingredients

- 1 cup (240ml) unsweetened Strawberry Juice
- 1 scoop (28g) Chocolate Protein Powder
- ½ cup (120ml) Strawberry Yogurt
- 1 teaspoon (5ml) unsweetened Cocoa Powder
- Sweeten to taste

Directions

Pour the strawberry juice and protein powder in your blender bottle and shake well until the protein powder is completely dissolved.

Add the remaining ingredients to the protein powder mixture and shake thoroughly until all ingredients are evenly blended together.

Note: calories may vary slightly due to brands and other recipe modifications.

Cinnamon Pie Shake

The simple ingredients to this shake make for a wonderfully tasting drink. The use of banana and banana cream pie yogurt provide a great tasting, smooth and creamy shake. This shake not only tastes great, but it is also packed with nutrients and proteins which makes it an ideal drink to end your day.

Makes: 1 *Serving*
Preparation Time: 5 *Minutes*
466 Calories per serving

Ingredients

- ½ cup (240ml) unsweetened Organic Coconut Milk
- 1 scoop (28g) Protein Powder
- ½ cup (120ml) Banana Cream Pie Yogurt
- 1 teaspoon (5g) Cinnamon Powder
- ½ of a large Banana Mashed

Directions

Pour the coconut milk and protein powder in your blender bottle and shake well until the protein powder is completely dissolved.

Add the remaining ingredients to the protein powder mixture and shake thoroughly until all ingredients are evenly

blended together.

Note: calories may vary slightly due to brands and other recipe modifications.

Fruity Tango Shake

The exotic flavor of mango combines with the health enhancing blueberry juice beautifully. The addition of lemon juice adds a lovely bite to this shake which has great texture from the added pecan meal.

Makes: *1 Serving*
Preparation Time: *5 Minutes*
492 Calories per serving

Ingredients

- ½ cup (120ml) unsweetened Blueberry Juice
- ½ cup (120ml) unsweetened Mango Juice
- 1 scoop (28g) Vanilla Protein Powder
- 1 teaspoon (6ml) Lemon Juice
- ¼ cup (38g) Pecan Meal

Directions

Pour the blueberry juice, mango juice and protein powder in your blender bottle and shake well until the protein powder is completely dissolved.

Add the remaining ingredients to the protein powder mixture and shake thoroughly until all ingredients are evenly blended together.

Note: calories may vary slightly due to brands and other recipe modifications.

Cherry Berry Shake

This deliciously sweet shake will energize everyone who tastes it. The antioxidants and flavonoids provided by the use of honey makes this a wonderfully healthy shake as well.

Makes: 1 Serving
Preparation Time: 5 Minutes
458 Calories per serving

Ingredients

- 1 cup (240ml) unsweetened Cherry Juice
- 1 scoop (28g) Vanilla Protein Powder
- ½ cup (120ml) Fat-free Triple Berry Yogurt
- 2 tablespoon (30g) Almond Butter
- Honey to taste

Directions

Pour the cherry juice and protein powder in your blender bottle and shake well until the protein powder is completely dissolved.

Add the remaining ingredients to the protein powder mixture and shake thoroughly until all ingredients are evenly blended together.

Note: calories may vary slightly due to brands and other recipe modifications.

Spinach Banana Shake

This shake combines the great tastes and health benefits of banana and spinach. This nutritious and protein packed drink will revitalize all who are feeling the after effects of a hard day's work.

Makes: 1 Serving
Preparation Time: 5 Minutes
208 Calories per serving

Ingredients

- ½ cup (120ml) unsweetened Almond Milk
- 1 scoop (28g) Protein Powder
- 1 tablespoon (15g) Organic Spinach Powder
- ½ of a large Banana, mashed
- Sweeten to taste

Directions

Pour the milk and protein powder in your blender bottle and shake well until the protein powder is completely dissolved.

Add the remaining ingredients to the protein powder mixture and shake thoroughly until all ingredients are evenly blended together.

Note: calories may vary slightly due to brands and other recipe modifications.

Spiced Raspberry Shake

The delicate taste of cinnamon in this shake wonderfully complements the rich flavor of the raspberries. This shake, has the added benefits from the addition of cottage cheese and could be described as a desert in a drink!

Makes: 1 Serving
Preparation Time: 5 Minutes
342 Calories per serving

Ingredients

- 1 cup (240ml) unsweetened Raspberry Juice
- 1 scoop (28g) Protein Powder
- ½ cup (120ml) Fat-free Cottage Cheese
- Dash of ground Cinnamon
- Sweeten to taste

Directions

Pour the raspberry juice and protein powder in your blender bottle and shake well until the protein powder is completely dissolved.

Add the remaining ingredients to the protein powder mixture and shake thoroughly until all ingredients are evenly blended together.

Note: calories may vary slightly due to brands and other recipe modifications.

Apple Spinach Shake

There is no better way to round off a great tasting dinner than with the sweetness of an apple. This shake combines this sweetness, and goodness, with a peach aftertaste. The addition of spinach ensures you receive a healthy dose of proteins, vitamins and iron.

Makes: *1 Serving*
Preparation Time: *5 Minutes*
293 Calories per serving

Ingredients
- 1 cup (240ml) unsweetened Apple Juice
- 1 scoop (28g) Protein Powder
- 1 tablespoon (15g) Organic Spinach Powder
- ¼ cup (60ml) Peach Yogurt
- Sweeten to taste

Directions
Pour the apple juice and protein powder in your blender bottle and shake well until the protein powder is completely dissolved.

Add the remaining ingredients to the protein powder mixture and shake thoroughly until all ingredients are evenly blended together.

Note: calories may vary slightly due to brands and other recipe modifications.

Chocobana Shake

This chocolate and banana shake will give you a vitamin and protein boost after dinner. Your whole family will love the combination of tastes in this drink and may even demand more!

Makes: *1 Serving*
Preparation Time: *5 Minutes*
269 Calories per serving

Ingredients

- 1 cup (240ml) Skim Milk
- 1 scoop (28g) Chocolate Protein Powder
- ½ of a large Banana, mashed
- 1 teaspoon Unsweetened Cocoa Powder
- 2 tablespoon (15g) Ground Chia Seeds

Directions

Pour the skim milk and protein powder in your blender bottle and shake well until the protein powder is completely dissolved.

Add the remaining ingredients to the protein powder mixture and shake thoroughly until all ingredients are evenly blended together.

Note: calories may vary slightly due to brands and other recipe modifications.

16

SHAKE UP YOUR LIFE!

Unquestionably, the overall health benefit of using protein powders to enhance our overall well-being is innumerable. Moreover, preparing healthy shakes from your blender shaker bottle is a welcome creativeness to protein powder consumers. With this recipe book, you'll be equipped with a useful resource and a variety of healthy and delectable protein shake recipes that are prepared using the popular shaker bottle.

Before my discovery of the blender shaker bottle, I was struggling to maintain an interesting and healthy protein rich lifestyle. For weight loss reasons, I had to find an easy way to incorporate more protein in my diet. Interestingly, the blender shaker bottle has helped me to easily achieve my health goals. Consequently, by using a combination of healthy ingredients with my protein powder, I have truly experienced remarkable health benefits. As I tell everyone, I now have a better body since I began to use these protein powder shake recipes—and that's something that money can't buy!

I thank you for choosing my recipe book. If this book has been helpful to you in any way, I would appreciate if you would let other readers know about it. I invite you to join me and countless others on an exciting journey to better health—shake up your life!

Happy Shaking,
Beth Harper

Printed in Great Britain
by Amazon

33116136R00102